COLD CHAOS

Stories from a North

NATHALIE GUILBEAULT

Montreal Publishing Company

COLD CHAOS, Stories from a North—1st edition, 2025

ISBN: 978-1-998353-07-1

Editor: Christian Fennell

Book Cover by Nelligan Design

Art by Christine Montague—christinemontague.com

Contents

Preface

DAY IN AND DAY out, it stretches before me: the long, narrow lake Massawippi, located in North Hatley, my companion for the past three years. I like to think I have been its companion, too. Another bystander of our shared movements. The Abenaki people tell us it is a lake filled with an abundance of clear water. Clearer thinking for me, yes—I am a February baby, after all—about my past, memories I chose to marvel at, right here, for the curious. To my complete surprise, winter, cold and humid, talked to me. I listened to what it had to say, what it was helping dig out—and stories emerged, auto-fictive in essence. And not.

This collection is not meant to form a historical account of the blue El Dorado this period was considered by many to be. It simply steeps inside imagination's cold well while winking at life's quiet truths. This collection is a way out, a river's mouth from which fresh and dead leaves flow.

My adolescent years were spent in James Bay during the execution of one of the world's largest hydroelectric projects, a period of my life I recall with rare lucidity. A golden age of sorts—my father's, a pioneer of the Quebec North, as well. This sentiment, like the images that light them, is vivid in its holding of this time, a feeling of freedom and hope and worry—matched only by the birth of my children. The birth of meanings. Stories, witnesses that speak, telling me I was there. The young woman I was, her mind caught in the taiga's grip, and the adults they held hostage. And, of course, they held her, too.

Not all witnesses are reliable, life has taught you and I. And yet they are necessary to our survival. Reminders of what we didn't see or thought we had; of who we were, and how far we never came. Witnesses can help us erase as much as expose.

Pain. Joy. Truth.

To them, I say: I am still here. I remember—the beauty and the foul. Like you—maybe?

For better and for worse.

What usually has the strongest psychic effect on a child is the life the parents have not lived. —*Carl Jung*

Jean. Pauline. Geneviève.

Adeline

Look at her. See her, won't you? For her sake.

Someone needs to.

She is sleeping in her bed, a curled, small body clinging to a light blanket. Too light to fight the cold floating in the room. Her left thumb tickles the inside of her palate as she rubs the bridge of her nose with her index finger, sucking security in. No light cast on her, and inside her chest, more obscurity; a child's turmoil needing to rise. Was it the wind that called to her that stormy night—to open her eyes, stand and walk away from her little self—to where? The fiery winter blowing on Labrador land, a land she knows nothing about. The map to a treasure chest. A quest, morphing inside her little heart.

Barefoot, she walks the short corridor to the entrance door. No one had thought to lock the door. No one, for only Mother is there. Daddy—gone far from home. A dam to build. A dyke to inspect. A wife to flee.

Outside, the howling is soft, yet constant. A howling there, inside her head, too.

Her pink flannel nightgown, white lace at the collar, is waving around her knees. In the middle of the front yard, she stands, half-dressed. Over-exposed. Snowbanks, her walls. Nighttime, a hand. The little girl is facing the other trailers located across her street, her short auburn hair tossed by the rapid snowfall, her cheeks burnt red. She stares yet does not see, does not feel, until her bare feet start to scream. Her toes, too.

A hand to her arm, and the mother's squeeze is hard, the pull back to her home just as well. Back in her bed, waiting: A cover that covers nothing but good dreams. A blanket that crushes.

This could be her story.

And I ask myself, how was it she heard my steps?

I don't know.

And sometimes, I don't believe she did—come to me, knowingly. So unlike her. Then and now. Maybe this mother had been sleepwalking, as I had, to me, the sub-conscious, the seat of her instincts that hadn't died—not yet—and saving me. Or maybe it was to save herself. That is often all I can believe. From the world's eye that would be thrown upon her.

All I know is that the longing has been long.

To be held.

Never satisfied or answered.

Still to this day.

Between Dog & Wolf

MICHIMAKAU'S TONGUE HUNG SIDEWAYS, batted by the wind, and the little girl looked at her, her hand resting on the dog's coat. The girl tilted her small face against the same wind—the same breeze, now quickening. She smiled. A late July day, a day belonging to the cold summers of this land, dusk about to surround them, the sun coming from a reliable west, behind the forest of larch and black spruce. Between dog and wolf—its own thing, like this man, father to the girl, and he pointed to the sky, just like Michi.

He loosely held the throttle, his eyes squinting as they hovered over the water, searching for the ridge of the woodland. Speeding back to where they had left the Suburban truck in the morning, his mind appearing empty—the quiet void inside his bliss. They had spent the day fishing on the Meo River, an offshoot of the Caniapiscau River, and now, five kilometers from shore, they were returning home, the bottom of the fifteen-foot Zodiac filled with wiggling trout.

She stood at the front of the boat, riding point, looking ahead, sureness inside her young mind: this complicity, bountiful, and boundless—of being held in these moments like this; of leaning into the elements that embraced her. She craved it. Like her father. Her fingers in the water, not resisting the current, its glacial feel, accepting of this world that would forever be with her.

That day.

A red dot in the distance—what? An ill-placed balloon heaving? It could have been anything, the man would later share. I could not have seen—looked away, dismissed it. He didn't, and he decided to investigate, lowering the front of the Zodiac until it kissed the hard rippling of the gray river.

The dusk was there and as they fled through its falling, they saw—something? Her eyes widened. It's capsized! she yelled.

Throttling down, tossed by the water, the man prudently maneuvered the inflatable closer to the canoe. He grabbed the handle located on its side, and as he pulled the small boat to him, Michi, tail up and body alert, placed her front paws on the bow of the boat. Grab her collar, her father called, or else she'll jump onto the canoe, and we don't need that trouble, too.

In silence they looked on, trying to dissect, gray from gray, ripple from ripple, until the sound of Michi compelled them to follow her gaze—an impatient whine. Forty feet from where they had stopped, the hint of movement broke the river's shakes. A head bouncing, an arm like a small hand, fighting. There, she yelled, pointing.

They sped up, stopping a few feet from the man. The boat in neutral, its motor returning water into the river, the sounding of a rush; of a strange stillness. He was colored, his lips, his face, and shivering, glossy eyes pointed to the sky, the man holding, as best he could, a burnt-orange floating jacket.

Dad ...

I know.

Turning to his daughter, he told her to remain at the stern of the Zodiac, that he needed her to steady the boat. See that dark spot over there? Aim for it, sweetie.

Directing his attention to the water, he looked at the man. Give me your hand, he yelled as he extended his arm to the man's exposed hand. The man in the water stared at the face looking down at him, an expression of shock carved on his own beginning to let go, and he slowly tried to unfold his arm and grab the helping hand. Several attempts and their fingers finally interlocked into a slippery connection.

With his knees set against the rubber of the boat, the father pulled against the current; against the man's exhaustion, and he pulled until he recognized resistance he would not be able to overcome. An unexpected weight. Fuck, he yelled, spotting a fishing rod floating near them, were you fly-fishing? The man blinked. Are you wearing fucking thigh waders? With teeth clattering and unable to speak, the man in the water nodded, yes. The tackle box, get my knife! he shouted to her. Now. We'll never be able to bring him inside the boat if I don't cut the straps latched to his waist. Just exactly how? the father thought. Continue steering the boat, he said. I need to go in.

The girl obeyed, muted by the colors slicing the waters. Orange and violet, she would forever remember—the colors of imminent death.

He removed his boots, and his coat, and sliding his body into the water, knife in hand, he swam closer to the man. His face, he thought. We don't have much time. Hypothermia is setting in. How long have you been in the water? The man's lips were shining and blue and he couldn't speak. Don't worry, I'll get you out. But I need to unhook the straps from you. Okay? You're too heavy with these on. You understand? What's your name? he yelled as he felt for the belt. The man's lips slowly moved. Louder, I can't hear you. Syllables, faint, barely audible. Michael? All right, Michael. I can't see anything right now, the water's too dark. I can't feel your belt either. I need to go in, okay? And don't let go of your vest, hang on tight.

From nowhere—everywhere?—the sound of a splash came. The sound of Michi falling between the men—the dog now being carried away by the river's current.

Michi! she yelled. Michi!

Startled, the man had let go of his vest and was sinking, his hands searching for the body underneath him.

The girl saw her father's mouth—just his mouth! The vest, the father yelled to his daughter as he pushed and kicked away from the man. The vest! Throw me the vest!

The dog, Dad!

Later! The fucking vest, sweetie! And the rope as well!

Where is it?

Underneath the back seat. Quick!

He moved to where the bobbing head was, and quickly finding the man's arm, he tried to pull more of the body above the surface. Calm down, and listen to me, he shouted through the wind, the vest his daughter had thrown, landing next to him. The cold of the water setting in, he tried guiding the man's arm through one of the vest's holes, and he yelled more, to stop grabbing him, to stop fighting him. Do you understand me? And with his eyes locked on the man's mouth, he heard—this whimpering: I was not alone.

What do you mean?

—wife.

And with more sorrow to push back against, he said, all right, Michael, and he scanned the water around him. But right now, it's just you and me, and I can't get you in the boat. You understand that? I've got a rope here and this is what's going to happen. I'm going to tie it around your chest, right below your arms, and I'm going to pull you in. I'm going to tow you. Okay?

The man, closing his eyes, said, I want to sleep.

No, you don't, Michael. Keep your eyes open. You got kids?

Two girls, he whispered.

Okay. While I pull, you look up, all right? The sky. Think of them. Just think of them.

The water now feeling colder, he began sluggishly to swim back to the boat, dragging the rope behind him.

Her little hands reaching, helping him. Hurry up, Dad, and put your coat back on. I can barely see Michi from here. We have to leave.

The river and the skies, a unity soon to be one, and while putting on his coat he watched his daughter throttle up. Looking back at the man, he heard her yell—there! Michi!

Against a duotone of darkness, huddled in her parka, the young girl gripped the throttle hard, her eyes guessing, her mind unsure. Through the engine's noise, her father's words, meant to quell—reassure: We're almost there. Michi can make it.

The waters of a July that felt like a wintery sea, embracing him harder, the coldness of it now unfelt, and the man continued to look up. Above him, mercury was running from the sun, wanting to go to sleep, too. And now, inside the skies, staring at him, his daughters' eyes.

Slow down, the father told his daughter, we're almost there, see? Through the falling obscurity, he looked back, we're about to shore up, Michael. One minute, he yelled through the engines' rush.

They slid the boat onto the gravelly beach, the dog waiting, shaking water from its coat. The father jumped from the boat and yelled to his daughter, get on the CB, and grabbing the rope he pulled as he ran into the water until he reached the man. He untied the rope from the man's chest. Call the hospital—tell them we are at the Meo. They'll know where to send the chopper. And start the truck. We need heat. The blankets are in the back.

Holding the man in his arms, he looked down at him, we made it, man. We made it. Look.

There were tears in the man's eyes. Inside of them, a mix of deception and sadness. The man's eyes sank into the father's, and as he closed them one last time, he said, I did it, man.

I pushed her.

People Beyond The Horizon

From where he stood, just behind the Bell helicopter he had just stepped out of, thirty-two-year-old Lucca Bartolucci quickly understood. What had unfolded—the horror of it. One of the four heads had been sliced a third of the way, above the eyes, a rogue lobotomy; a buzz cut gone wrong. The other three had been sectioned at the mouth, just about, bottom lips left with a tongue, blue and long. Hair attached to scalps. Human pellets littering the snow.

Behind the crashed chopper, the George River, a liquid sonority bordered by icy snow. Snow reddened by blood—the surveyors'; they had been tasked with conducting field surveys for the soon-to-be constructed houses the natives had negotiated with the government. They were returning home for the holidays. A strange yet poetic tableau, and the meaning of the river resonating with it. River without trees, the Naskapi say. Where there are no trees lies more blood, Bartolucci thought as he approached the scene. We now know why they were missing, he said to his pilot, as they walked knee-deep in the snow, stepping over the helicopter's tilted blades.

It landed off to the side, the pilot said. On a rock, just here. And they must have panicked, gotten off too quickly. A fire would do that, he continued, pointing to the soot painting the inside of the cabin.

So it seems, Doctor Bartolucci said as he kneeled by a body, staring at the disfigurement. He stood, looking around. Where's the pilot?

I don't understand either.

Doctor Bartolucci turned to where the pilot was now staring. An old native, a Naskapi man, was holding in his arms a shaky man, his mouth open, yet soundless. The missing pilot.

We got him, Doctor Bartolucci said as he approached the old man. Let's call some help to get the bodies out. Nodding to the old native, he sat in front of the pilot. Good man, he said, checking his vital signs. You're going to be fine. He helped the man to his feet, again nodding to the old native, snow whipping the air. The winds have picked up. A storm is coming our way. Come on, he said, you need to walk faster. And for a moment, his body leaning into the wind, he cursed the land, whispering to no one: in wintertime lies death's cool silk.

He came back to his trailer—a bachelor pad located beside the hospital he had helped design, turmoil behind his eyes. A known sight. He removed his outerwear, then, drawing a bath, he stripped naked, sliding inside the plastic tub, and he thought of what he had seen that day. The randomness of it. He propped his legs up, placing his heels along the tub's edge.

Images of the day came back to him. Death was life, and that was fine. Live life when you live. Death when you die. Makes sense, he thought, sliding further into the water.

Water covering his head, he closed his eyes, thought of her, and wished for a silhouette to appear—the shape of her that had been hovering over him, a loop inside his mind, ever since he had stepped onto Naskapi land, four years before. Each night, the same piercing dream coming, yet never lulling: She is moving in the middle of a snow field, century-old black spruce, her audience, standing, immobile, winds not touching them, touching her—only her; she sways with grace, her gestures refined, her eyes poised on a faraway line, responding to the cold currents, and as she sways, she talks to him, but he cannot hear, seeing only her lips moving, her face slowly being erased by the winds.

Loneliness, unfriendly and untamed, the truest of companions, yet what haunted him most was the possibility of living a life parallel to that of a being meant for him, and yet not knowing. Not meeting. Never touching. The absurdity of it.

When he woke, Doctor Bartolucci thought of hope, and of his arrival to this place that had no resemblance to the country he had left behind.

I just want to feel. I want the permanence of it.

Closing his eyes again, sleep about to revisit, a river appeared to him. Wait, it told him. Wait.

———

Following the third and final curtain fall, second soloist Natasha Romanova waddles, her feet flat to the ground, the tip of her toes aching, her right ankle throbbing.

Inside the dressing room, the usual after show routine, a sweat scented choreography of its own where the Soviet ballerinas whine and cry, a feminine voice, insistent in its stringency, reminding them of what they were not. Would never be. Perfect.

The voice fades, and in silence, with her head down, she rubs her ankle. Her temples, too. She undresses, meticulously hanging Ekaterina's costume on the troupe's rack. Silence is in her veins. Goodbye Kitty. Goodbye Anna Karenina.

The corps de ballet gathers in silence at the entrance of the performance hall. It is close to midnight, the lights in the lobby dim, the cleaning staff nonchalantly going about its duties. Nervous, Natasha sits on the edge of a resting water fountain and takes out a pack of cigarettes from her duffle bag and starts peeling the packaging off as the ballet master appears. All right girls and boys, she says, looking ahead at the revolving doors where an old man waits for the troupe to leave so he can lock the doors until the morning, time to leave for the hotel. Natasha, standing, slides her pack inside her coat pocket.

The return is brisk, the pace uneven, the young women, their necks twisted to the night, their eyes lapping the many store windows filled with things only heard about, never possessed. Here and there, they stop. Googly eyes. Hungry for nothing home has to offer them. Any of them.

Walking the city sidewalk, Natasha feels more pain clinging to her ankle and climbing to the back of her knee. More acute than usual. A sign, she tells herself. The shelf-life soon-to-be dead. And she looks at the master, the stiffness of her being, her jawline, too, tense, yet saggy, and threatening to drop further, her face wrinkled by the wrong type of excesses; of deficiencies. I love you, she hears herself say, and I know you made me. I just can't go on. Feeling the weight of something pressing on her shoulders, the master turns around and stares back. Natasha, she simply says, Natasha, she repeats. And turning her back, moving into the city night-lights, the woman continues to walk.

Once back inside the hotel room Natasha shares with three other girls, she quickly showers and slides into her jeans and sweatshirt. As she puts her boots back on, the throbbing of her ankle makes her wince. She takes a breath, then tells the girls she needs to fetch some ice. For all of us, she says, pointing at one of the girl's feet. They are red and swollen. Bleeding, too. No one looks up. Absorbed by an episode of Charlie's Angels playing on the television set, no one notices she should have been barefoot to fetch some ice, that she shouldn't have grabbed a coat from the closet before leaving the room. Carrying no ice bucket. Instead, settled against her chest, hanging from her shoulders, a small duffle bag. Inside it, her essentials: ballerina shoes; bodysuits; tutus.

She steps into the elevator—the room is located on the floor below hers, and she presses seven. The piped music above her, James Last, loud, vapid. Once the doors close, feeling the elevator drop a short drop, she looks at the image of her reflected by the worn-out metal facing her. The distortion makes her smile. She looks old, as though a part of her has melted onto itself. Her face, acutely oblong. A death like oblong. Her eye bags, dark and veiny, elongating almost to her nose. When the doors reopen, she straightens her posture and walks slowly to room 717.

The woman hears the steps coming and stopping at the door, the knocking about to be heard. She had sensed it. From where she comes from, everyone senses it, the push—not the pull—to leave. Everyone nurturing the same dream. She did, too, at some point. Then, for some, like her, fed by the possibility of failing, of being caught, the point of no return does return. To its staring point—home is home, even if mud season ends up swallowing all the other ones.

She knows who is behind the door. Not hiding anymore. And so, she takes her time, letting it assault her with its many reels. One in particular, and the smells of sewage, rotten cabbage, and dry blood bundle up, filling her nostrils. The Siberian orphanage.

The ballet master finally opens the door, takes Natasha's hand, and bringing it to her lips, whispers she is sorry. But that she understands. Natasha nods, whispering she, too, is sorry. Sorry she must go. Thank you, Sonia, she mouths.

The women stare at one another, the master understanding a mother will do anything to save her child. From her coat pocket, she slides it out. There is no more time, Natasha, she says, as she hands the girl her passport; surprised by the looseness of her voice, she tells her to go. Now. Quickly. And closing the door, the woman reaches for the chain, locking the door.

Natasha rushes toward the exit door, down the seven flights of stairs. At each landing, she looks up, stilling, expectant of trouble. Each time, nothing.

Once at the final landing, she pushes the door, walking quickly through the lobby and onto the city streets. Continue to the left, she tells herself, her hand toying with the address she has written on a piece of paper tucked inside her hand. Then another left, then walk for five miles. She has memorized the route, and feeling the crinkling of the paper inside her hand makes her feel less alone.

As she hurries along the city's laneways, breathless, a sharp sound comes up from her feet.

At the end of an alley, she stops and places her back against the wall of a small building. Slowly, she slides to the ground, a hand probing the inside of her boot. Underneath, the threat of a bone about to pierce skin. Negating the pain, biting her lower lip, she looks to the left, to a park, narrow and long. She stands, careful not to put excess weight on the injured ankle, and she limps to the bench closest to her. There, she sits. There, she falls asleep. Upon waking, she looks up. The morning has already settled in the moon's light. And fear is still alive inside of her, yet somehow, she knows all would work out. It must.

I slept in the park for two days, the Indian summer my shelter. The pain had settled in a no man's land, oscillating between two borders, unable to commit to a side. Not moving was the only way to survive, the only way to keep agony at a safe distance.

For two days I contemplated the choice I had set in motion: to leave—exactly what? My body was worn out, my foot no better than that of a lame horse's. I had no choice. They would have put me out to pasture, my love, the many versions of Russian pasture. Master—Sonia, too.

I lifted myself from the bench, slowly walking the last mile to my destination.

When I stepped into the offices of The Royal Canadian Mounted Police, located downtown Montreal, the bone had won, protruding through the skin. I don't know if it was the state of despair my face wore—a grayish tint, I would be told, later, around which my tangled braids towered, or the blood-soaked boot I was dragging across their linoleum floor, but the uniformed man seated at the reception was quick to act.

The dialogue was sparse, encumbered by my little knowledge of both French and English. Yet, through the staccato of my words, and encouraged by the kindness in his eyes, I told him returning to the homeland meant death, morsels of death reliable in their punctuality.

Then, before thinking of you; of us—I fainted.

———

From her hospital bed, she opens her eyes. The room is bright, the sun bleaching the walls' yellowish tint. She props herself up, squints. A familiar pain, just then. Of course. Her eyes widen, and when they do, she sees her right foot encased in white plaster. She sees her blackened toes exposed, the absence of nails. One of ballet's many gifts. She closes her eyes, recalling: the last performance; Sonia; the walk; the officer. I've left, she whispers. I've escaped. Fatigue shoots up behind her eyes, and she slides her body back onto the mattress, closing her eyes.

When she wakes, the day has gone, stolen by the fall's love for early dusks. She sits up, sees the clock hanging on the wall. 5:30 p.m. Slowly, her eyes alert, she looks at the empty hospital bed across the room; at the wheelchair stationed by her bed; at the newspaper clipping placed on her side table. She will never know who placed it there. For her to see. Her heart sinks. The photo of Sonia is on the front page of the local newspaper. Underneath an old photo of the fallen star, written in large letters, she slowly reads what her mind slowly deciphers: Soviet ballerina found dead on her seat, inside the airplane bringing her and her troupe home. Natasha grabs the paper, her eyes watery. The carotid artery has been slit, she can decipher. A suicide, it reads.

More numbness coming, doubt, too.

The truest of mothers is gone.

It took well over two years for my case to be processed, my love—you must hear me?—for my life to find an allure I could claim my own. To live with the thought of Sonia in my head. During this time, I remained in Montreal, living with a family of Jewish Russians I met while at the hospital. Surprising to the doctors, my foot's open fracture mended quickly—the miracle of youth, and I was able to pursue ballet with the Canadian National Ballet, moving to Toronto, the audition easy to obtain, easy to pass. Russia after all, can open some doors.

For five years, I danced—Giselle, Swan Lake, Romeo and Juliet, Cinderella, Sleeping Beauty—blending only with the corps de ballet for my days as a semi-soloist had already been well consumed by another life. I was now twenty-five years old. Old to the world that had chosen me as its human. Sonia was never too far from my time there, a ghost I spoke to every now and then. And will I be just another ghost to you, as well? I wonder.

There was something flaccid about my relationships to the other dancers—it wasn't lifting. I had learned English. I had learned French. And yet, there was an uncrossable bridge. They spoke to me from afar, another place. The distance was there, tall. The other side. I, too, to be fair, had remained elsewhere, hesitant, living far away from where I had chosen to live. My mind, a compartmentalizing artist. It slowly had sneaked inside my head, on me like a late afternoon shadow. Long. Towering. Uncomfortable numbness.

I try to fight it. Everyday.

Follow me, my love, my story, I say.

The day before vacating the premises, a September day, wind-filled and cold, I dawdled by the community board located at the entrance of the dance studio. I had decided on going back to Montreal and live with the same Russian family. Lots of opportunity for you here, they told me. But going back felt wrong. Like a regression. Moving closer to the board, I scanned the many ads and announcements pinned to the corked slat. Nanny positions up for grabs. Room boarding. Ballet shoes for sale, tutus, too, used and new. Then, I smiled, at the image first—a cold, blinding white, pulling and hypnotic, a desert that belonged to a desolation my blood could make sense of, understand—then at the words.

Part-time ballet teacher wanted.

Location: James Bay.

Destination: you.

His eyes fluttered, his fingers poking the surface of the water.

A silence worming as if from a river's bed; water, deep, and not moving.

Inside, with her now, and he felt his body lift.

A low hovering.

From that time, on a faraway mind, a blur could remain.
Like the secrets that live inside a river.

Upon seeing the camp, its many rows of white trailers
planted inside the frozen gravelly ground and set against
a falling snow, Natasha knows she has made the right decision. The closest thing to home, she thinks, as she brings
an arm to her chest.

Suitcase in hand, she climbs the steps, unsure, walking
inside the dormitory, one of the few the camp has allocated
to its women employees. A humming greets her as she
walks in; a busy one. It is 6 p.m. A few women already
have returned from their cafeteria dinner and are readying
themselves for some television watching in the common
area. She walks in her room, the first one to the right as
one comes into the trailer, and tired from the eight-hour
plane trip—a milk run made of seven layovers—remaining
dressed, she lets herself fall onto the bed.

The noise shakes her up. Laughter, mostly. Feminine
laughter. She stands and walks to the door. Peeking her
head through the opening, she sees three women hanging inside the corridor. Turning her head to her, a short,
black-haired woman returns the stare. Natasha Romano-

va, she smiles. The other two women, their backs to the wall, look at her, too. You finally got here, they say in tandem. More laughter, and they walk to her, pushing the door inside her room, her with it. Let's get some vodka, the dark-haired one says. And leaning toward Natasha, she whispers, my name is Pam. Pam Knox. I'm the camp barber. Her eyes meet, and while Pam's unsettle hers, Natasha smiles a tired smile, and says, yes girls, vodka sounds perfect.

***

Winters, true and fierce, knocked—an eternity of constants—and the camp administration, acquiescing to the women's demands, had brought me to sucker punch boredom from their reality—something to do other than snowshoe, cross-country, work. Drink. I signed a one-year teaching contract, a first one: November to November.

I held the classes inside the community centre—two trailers that had been joined together, located at the edge of the camp. Inside the tight space, there were no mirrors for students to gage themselves by, no bars to exercise from, only the back of metal chairs to hang onto. To my surprise, a piano was brought in, prompting one of the women to forgo ballet and become our pianist.

Every evening, except for weekends, from seven to ten, about twelve women, all coming from the camp, not the village—women there, mostly stay-at-home wives, had their own activities, and despised the single women, secretaries for the most part, a threat, who worked with their husbands—regularly sauntered into my classroom. Dressed in leggings and checkered shirts, others in shorts and tees—a funny-looking bunch—they came ready to sweat, ready to dance. My way. I was tough. Loving to be so. And it came quickly, the answer to a question that had puzzled me from the moment I had arrived—why was I really here? To soothe, I came to realize, the classes a haven, a place away from the male eye. I had transformed into a hideaway.

The full year unfolded without pause—without wanting to pause. Sonia, a thought I had managed to stow away. But something wasn't right with me—I just didn't know what it was.

Unlike most everyone at camp, I had no one, no family, pulling me back to the city, and so, during this first year, I remained on site, accepting secretarial temp jobs sporadically throughout the year, on top of giving ballet classes during wintertime. The money was great—exiled from civilization, everyone's pay-check was a greased-up one. Following a short hiatus—I didn't teach during the summer—October came around, ballet season about to pursue its merry mission.

I remember the day, its morning, and you would, too, my love, for you know mornings deliver mundanities we all like to surrender to; seek—nothing can happen to anyone inside those moments. The hot hit of the shower's water on your skin. The first sip of coffee while facing the sun. Your lover's lips pressed against yours as you prepare to leave for work. The day will be good, you think, *has* to be good. That the ordinary will act as a shield; that it is a shield.

And my morning was carrying the day's secret.

That day, after renewing the terms of my contract, while walking on the utilidors linking the camp's trailers together, I stumbled and fractured my ankle.

That is when I met you.

It looks good, he says, his hands over her ankle. The ankle is white, with just a hint of yellow still lingering where the main bruise had initially formed. It's been two months, he continues, as he flexes the joint. It doesn't even hurt, does it?

She wiggles her toes, unsure. I can still dance, Lucca, no?

Of course, Natasha. His eyes screw into hers. He smiles. Your hair, what happened?

Embarrassed, she turns away, bringing her fingers to the dried-up curls. This girl at my dorm. Said she could do it, said she was good, that she had taken a beauty class in high school. A half-assed technical degree. Fucking Pam, she thinks. I should have known better than to trust her, Lucca.

Pam Knox, he says.

Right, you're her doctor, everyone's doctor.

Why did you … you know, trust her?

I don't know. I guess she has her way of getting what she wants. It's in those eyes of hers, practiced eyes. They seem so trustworthy.

People can fool you …

She pauses, looking straight at her ankle. I watched her at the club last weekend. Again. It's quite fascinating. The way she lures those idiots. Says she will land herself a guy with enough money, a guy who will make all her dreams happen. That she wants babies, needs them. To breathe.

I can see what you mean. In the medical field, we call them devouring mothers. They take only. Give in appearance, only. He brings a finger to his mouth. Shh. I can't say more.

Poor guy, she whispers. Whoever falls in her trap—those eyes, and believes her deceptions, the ride's gonna be a rough one. Unforgiving.

There seems to be more, though. I can see that. Something else ...

Her eyes became watery. Gesturing as though a fly was surrounding her head, she whispers that the woman reminds her of someone. Sonia, she thinks. The failed pursuit of her pregnancies. Her only child, Natasha. The vulnerability, mostly.

And she burned your hair, he said with a large smile.

And she burned my hair.

He winks, his long lashes brushing the air, and he laughs, too. It grows back, he says with a wink, and pulling on the strand of hair brushing against her cheek. I know about these things. He looks at the calendar hanging on the wall across his desk, then lifts his eyes to hers. Tell you what, Miss Natasha, I must see a patient this week. A friend of mine. A member of the Naskapi tribe located near the mining town of Schefferville. Why don't you come with me?

Natasha slowly props her legs to her chest, scrunching the medical paper to her thighs. Turning, still seated, she lets her legs dangle, the cold air weaving between her toes, the cold air running through her body. Doctor Bartolucci is now hunched over at his desk, looking at the last X-ray of her foot. She studies him, his colored skin, his shock of dark hair, a lanky body always agitated, just as his mind has proven to be. A man that never stops moving. Lucca Bartolucci, a dentist as well as a general physician, was the wilderness' savior. This Italian aristocrat, raised in Switzerland, bartering a life of comfort for the rudeness of permanent winters, had become a thing in her life. For two months, now. Something undefined emerging. How long would I be gone for?

He swivels the chair, his feet pushing off the floor, and rolling it to where the examination table was. So, Miss Natasha, you *are* interested ...

Well, she starts, I haven't taken any breaks since I've been here...

He smiles, fingers circling both her ankles. Really? Then, I guess we need to change that ...

She smiles back at the small glimmer piercing through his eyes, inky and mat. It's Christmas time, anyway. So, yes, I say. I'm coming with you.

———

Seated behind him, mittened hands to his chest, Natasha nestles her bundled face into his parka. The snow is falling hard, the wind pushing onto them as the snowmobile speeds through the white-dotted curtain. Following the George River shore, looking at the landscape surrounding them, Russia comes to mind. Her Russia. The barren land of her birth, somewhere in Siberia. And Pam comes to mind. This obsession. The state of Pam. Her mind is barren, too, she thinks, yet no one sees it. Just me for I am trained to see and understand all that is poor of yielding. All that is dead.

The track they follow leads them to where the Naskapi live, a settlement the tribe has recently obtained from the government. A slum, Doctor Bartolucci had explained the week before. We should be ashamed. To have played with their lives without impunity. Making them live in filth and telling them it is a kingdom. A kingdom they should feel grateful to have.

Yes, she nods to herself. But she doesn't want to think about someone else's misery. She has her own to wonder about, untangle, and now is the time to empty her mind. She lets go, believing she is safe, secure, held by time, by faith, by fairness, and as she holds on to this strength, novel to its own existence, she closes her eyes.

He turns his head back, toward her, a breath hot, humid, catching the side of her face. We're almost there, he yells. Yes, she yells back, snow falling in her mouth. He presses harder on the accelerator, sending more snow into the air, his head filled with all the lives he has lost, and saved, he hopes. Knows—maybe—can this be her?

And will I save her, too?

He points ahead, and around them, nothing but empty space—hypnotic and hushing and so accessible to this will to surrender, century old spruce sometimes brushing against their sight, trunks like human arms, thin yet sturdy. Pushed around, but never surrendering. I know, she thinks, scanning the landscape, you isolated yourself by choice, from civilization, a Renaissance man of the north. Lucca, I can see now. Understand. This is who you were born to be.

The snowmobile slows to a stop. Come, he yells to her against the wind. Come quick. He takes her hand, and they walk through the snow, dragging their feet toward a beat-up tent made of old caribou skin, the sun still, overlooking the landscape, threatening to stay.

Stopping at the entrance of the tent, a female voice coming to them, she points to the five rows of houses located across from where they stand. Why doesn't he live there, with the other tribe members? she asks.

Because, Natasha, it is not his home. He takes her hand. Follow me inside.

A grassy smell greets them as they enter, and they see an old woman standing, her face lost in a soft tension, and singing the healing magic of a trance.

A medicinal song, he says.

The sound of coughing, dry and unproductive, joins the rhythm. The tent, dimly lit by the presence of orange-spitting lanterns feels like the inside of a cave. She brings the scarf up to her nose.

The boiled bough of black spruce, he says, as he walks to the old man lying on a small cot opposite the entrance. Medicinal herbs.

Does it work?

Knees to the ground, he places a hand on the man's feverish forehead. Long gray hair escaping from the man's fur hat. Unruly white bristles of hair sprouting from a chin, long and narrow. I believe it can, he says. But medicine is more like art than science, even in my world. Come, Natasha. Sit with me.

Doctor Bartolucci turns to the old man. Awakened by their presence, the man's eyes are now open, his smile, faint. A face made of seasoned skin, and it tells of wisdom, of patience. Of resignation, too.

What does he have?

A soft, controlled breath. He is simply dying. Pneumonia.

Can you save him?

Ignoring her question, Doctor Bartolucci puts his mouth close to the man's ear, and in Naskapi dialect, staccato, and decisive in tone, tells the old man, about the life he has help save not so long ago, taking care of the pilot, for two weeks, by the river, that his turn to be saved has come. I cannot do anything for you here, old man. If you want to live, you must allow me to lift you to my hospital. There, I can save you.

The old man turns to him, looking intently at him, and Doctor Bartolucci sees the kindness moving inside a gaze where eyes too often blinded by snow had surrendered to nature's looking glass.

But here, you will die, Doctor Bartolucci continues softly. You and I know that.

The old man takes Bartolucci's hand in his, squeezing it with warmth. Then, it is decided. You can go. Me, Lucca, I will remain, here on my land. My body belongs to it. Like my spirit.

Doctor Bartolucci nods to the man, squinting water away from his eyes, this understanding soaked in humility. Time to go, he tells Natasha, as he stands, looking into his friend's quiet gaze. We'll be back in the morning.

Outside, night's cape, long and wide, and clouds hang low, lacy edges decipherable to the curious eye only. The hotel room is cold. The bed narrow. Sitting on the edge of the bed, facing the window, she stares at the paisley pattern of the curtains' fabric. I don't know why they even bother hanging them, she says mindlessly. It's always night this time of year. She pauses. You've known him for long?

From behind, he wraps his arms around her. Two years, he says. Since the chopper accident I told you about.

How is it you stayed in touch?

Settling beside her, he says the old man is the tribe's doctor. That he has taken a liking to his ways. I'm just interested. In people. In their beliefs. Their methods of living. Of healing.

There was a crucifix on the man's chest ...

The White Man's wake. But no. It's just a trinket left behind by the missionaries. Another bauble they collect. They don't believe in our god, you know, they simply allow others in, without judgment. No rituals mark their lives, either. Objects. Animals. These are their gods.

No religion ...

Their religion lies in the dreams they dream. That's where everything starts, he says, and ends. Inner voices that reveal the unconscious. Their compass to what makes sense. To them, the soul of a man is Man's only friend, his inner companion. Around here he is called MistaPeo—Great Friend.

Dreams—she thinks of Sonia. Of what her own nights write inside her mind. Childhood stories she has never shared with anyone.

Natasha ...?

I'm okay, she whispers back to him.

What are you thinking of?

To be honest, I try not to think so much these days. Because I think it's not safe for me to do so.

Thinking can be dangerous, he smiles, overthinking, that is. But something must feel like it can keep you safe ...

Her hand twirls the air in dismissal. Why are you here?

The question. Right. He scratches his chin, pauses. I left Italy. Left my bullshit family. I understood early on, when young, that I wanted to feel more. And I get that part of me. I understand myself. Understand there is more to life than the luxury of wanting nothing, for you have it all. I gave it all away, anyway.

That is why you are here. Living inside the luxury of essentials.

I think so.

Your question, now. She sways back and forth. Dancing, real, hardcore, bloody dancing, used to make me feel safe. The pain of it feeling so good. From when I was young, too, I guess I knew myself like you did. But now that I've stopped dancing, for real, that my body is healed ... I miss my pain.

You miss your pain?

I do. I think it's why Pam Knox is such a fascination for me. A lighthouse of self-destruction. I've seen her, in the bathroom, cutting herself. Deep cuts. She looks at him. You must have seen them.

He looks at her, nodding. The eyes have died, he thinks. Something retreating.

And how did you learn the language? she asks suddenly.

How? Made time for it, I guess. A language spoken by 1,000 people only. I'd say a good two years.

So why the interest?

Because I thought he was worth it. Something about him. I made room for something, somcone, I thought was meaningful.

Magic?

Maybe.

And now he is dying.

He let his head drop, chin to chest. Now he is dying.

Looking at him, she sees, the tiredness, a warrior's momentary lapse of everything. The buckling of resilience. She takes his hand, tells him it is time to lie some more, to get some rest. Come, she insists, beside me.

They meet for a first time, a strange yet soothing bloom, their body harboring answers waiting to be probed; by motion as much as word. The gift of this first touch, she slowly breathes in, aware she will never want to forget it. And nestled inside the warmth of a multicolored Naskapi blanket over which a caribou hide has been placed, the tandem moves as if one; a perfect audition; a lingering duo. Face-to-face, nose touching, he will wait a patient wait. Still.

———

The bath water is cold, and yet, you do not move, Lucca.
Because I am here with you.
Stay there like this.
Let me look at you.

———

Tell me, he says, your secret. She stares at him, this beauty carved inside each of his features, knowing that if she hears herself tell her tale, all will become too real, that once heard, her voice will become movement: She will return to her land, despite the fate that awaits the like of women and men like her. Defectors. It's not much of a secret, she finally says. Its weight is meaningful to me only, in its thinned-out complexity. I escaped here thinking my life would be better—and sometimes it is, the freedom, you know, but freedom comes at the cost of feeling you never belong, never will belong—so I could feel the same cold, thinking my bearings would be the same, if not similar. But no. And even if they were, it wouldn't be enough. I miss her, my land, Lucca. I miss hearing the tones and rhythms of my language. I miss the music my feet only want to dance to. It's as if I can't negate its pull, a request to blend inside its soil. I don't understand why I miss the harshness ... the pain ... I guess it's what I know. Body pain quiets, you know, the mind. My personal experience, she sighs, and through her tears she explains how she had been destined for a quick death, a baby placed inside a container of coal, the white of her eyes the distraction that had halted a miner from burying her with more coal, the shovel missing her small, gelatinous neck. Of how she had been sent to an orphanage, raised by a young woman who she had learned to call Mother. Sonia. The only way to survive the hardships this sad place was, and still is, for fifteen years, was to dance, Lucca. As if your life depended on it. A woman there, an ex-ballerina herself, saw us, understanding we had the goods, and wanting to make money ... She swallows. Sonia and I were sold to the Bolshoi, she let out, and Sonia remained by my side throughout those years. She helped me become a dancer worthy of the troupe. And my defecting to here killed her. Got her killed. I know it did. She looks at him, explaining more, atonement on her mind, and moves her head closer to his. Sleep, Natasha, sleep, he says. And remember that too much light shed on any life can also kill. That light, in excess, will draw the same fears absolute obscurity pours upon us, any of us.

He wakes up, he drags a hand to where her body should be. It isn't. He looks around. Her coat and boots are missing, her duffle bag still there, placed atop the dresser. He quickly slips into his clothes, convinced breakfast is waiting for them. He runs down the stairs to the hotel's small restaurant. It is Christmas morning after all.

Once outside, he hops onto the snowmobile. The hotel manager said Natasha had left early in the morning. That she had taken a pair of leftover cross-country skis and boots from the mudroom. That she wanted to ring Christmas in, on her terms.

The ride to her is slow. It hasn't snowed during the night, and it makes it easier for him to see the ski tracks she has left behind. The night's conversation is clinging to him: the resounding memory of skin; of lips; of hands—her voice. And he smiles when he recalls her feet, forever calloused, deformed, yet endearing to him. Eyes to the snow, he slows down, suddenly understanding, recognizing. He stops the snowmobile, follows the footsteps until they disappear—to the edge of the George River.

The local police and the town's people search, yet knowing she has gone, and too exhausted to go back home, to the camp, the fourth night, he walks to the old man's tent. When Doctor Bartolucci enters, eyes bloodshot, distress having carved new features on his face, the old man is sitting upright, hands to his chest. Waiting. The cough has gone away. So has the fever. You seem better, old man, he whispers, two fingers pressing the inside of the man's wrist. The old native nods, opaque eyes yet brilliant, and waits more. He motions for the young doctor to sit beside him and takes his hand. I had a dream, he starts, his voice clear. Your woman came to me, Lucca. She was twirling at the bottom of the river. And I know, you have seen her, too.

She was singing about her land, about the need to go home.

I had fallen asleep in the bathtub, forgetting where I was. Again. When I came to, the cold water rounding me, I stood, stepping onto the floor. Quickly, I slid into cleaner clothes, picking up the watch I had placed on the bathroom counter. It was midnight. Midnight at Christmas.

Walking the short distance to the hospital, I looked up. The northern lights were dancing above me. Soft and ethereal, pinks and reds. Waves. Visual music. It seemed to me they were drawing something—a round, lace-like shape. Dazed from the day, from the night—from images, vivid and confusing—I walked the stairs leading to the main office, and as I did, a song tickled the inside of my head. Okay, I whispered. Okay. I opened the door to the empty waiting area, walked to where the only occupied room was, pushing the plastic curtains aside. The pilot was seated, waiting for me. You're alive, I said to him, as I pulled a chair to his bedside. Delicately pulling the bandage off his head, I looked, smiled. It's only a flesh wound, man. You got lucky. The man's eyes, watery and bright, and he looked to me, unable to talk. I know, I said. About the loss. The shock. But you are alive. You made it, somehow. And stop crying, stop asking me why. Why? Why people come. Why people go.

No one ever knows. Not even why it is they remain.

But there are people who will come to stay. In your life. You will hear, see, signs of their permanent visiting. If you want to. All you can do is to wait, prepare—in spite, if not because: of moments like these.

Just then, a voice came, and I turned to it. Underneath the door frame, my nurse, Amy, was standing. There is a woman who just got here, funny accent and new to the camp, I think, she said, brought in by two drunken girls. Looks like they had a good go at it…

Right. What's the issue?

Looks like this one will be easy, Lucca. Easier.

Oh?

A simple, fractured ankle.

And from behind her, you appeared, a dreamer like me, a lucid one, I could tell, and you were limping, and I smiled when you smiled, and I thought how brilliant the day was going to be. My life, maybe too. I thought of the river, of the candor it carries. Of the certainties that live inside our wants.

Hi, Lucca, you said. Remember me?

Ungava Babe

JOHN BRODEUR BRINGS THE sugar bowl closer to him, pours what appears to be half its content into his cup of black tea. He stirs the syrupy liquid with his spoon, and no one notices he tucks the spoon between his arm and the side of his ribcage. And as he tells Adeline that he has a surprise for her, he slides the convex part of the hot steel against her fleshy triceps. Startled, she laughs, with him—a shared laughter, complicit, tenderizing the mood, for she knows, the mood always needs tenderizing around them. It's not about walking on eggshells; it's about walking as little as possible.

Can't believe you get me each time, she says, looking at him, gratefulness loosening her throat.

Mom told me you're off school for a while, said your sister is at her friend Julie's for the weekend.

Yay, she thinks. No Coco around for two days.

So, I've decided to bring you with me today.

The eggs on her plate are not scrambled enough, under-cooked, and she stops playing with their drool. She lifts her head. Really, Dad? Another chopper ride?

He shakes his head. No more of that, Adeline. And I fired those guys, you know. They wanted to impress you, and it could have killed us.

Great, Dad, wring the fun out of this place. Hovering and tilting two feet above an airstrip pretending to be racing a car, *that* was fun. Is Mom coming, too?

The voice is soft, as soft as Eva Brodeur's eyes have become. No, I'm not Adeline. I can't today.

Adeline looks at her father. Oh? Why not? It would be nice for her ...

No, not today, he says, looking at his wife. Next time, Eva. There's only room for two, and since Adeline is free ...

It's okay Johnny, next time. Maybe ...

A DC-3? Adeline asks, turning to her father.

It's not. Your ride is called Hercules this time, he replies, getting up. The only boyfriend you're allowed to date around here, he adds with a wink.

He walks to his wife and caresses her backside, brushes her cheek with his lips. Don't wait for us for dinner, Eva, we'll be eating in Fort-Chimo tonight. Before the flight back home.

Her mother's shoulders weaken, warmth climbing to her face. She tugs at the inside of her turtleneck. It is shiny and it is blue and each time she sees her wearing it, Adeline thinks of how beautiful she is. She doesn't quite know why she does, why the glittery fabric ignites her the way it does when looking at her. Maybe because these are the only lights that will ever come out of you, she thinks.

Air, Eva whispers, I need to breathe. She inhales, looks to the outdoor thermometer hanging outside the kitchen window. -35 C. And I'm burning up.

Brodeur pushes an eight-track inside the cassette tape player—Roger Whittaker's whistling floats inside the truck. Aware of the roads' trickiness, the man concentrates on keeping the truck's wheels aligned with the road. The ground ice, pale-blue and almost matching the day's sky, keeps him focused, as if he wants to know it better, its ridges, its traps.

The airport is almost empty, the last Convair of the day having just taken off. Aboard the propeller plane are fifty workers eager to go back home for their ten-day hiatus. Adeline flies it so often she knows the plane will be filled with thick blue smoke, inescapable and suffocating, with men barely capable of keeping their hands to themselves. Two months without relief in sight, or so little, transform

them into the beasts they need to be in order to tolerate the wilderness. Nature propping up nature, she often
thought, a puzzle fitting into itself. They come for the
money, Dad, she had once asked, but do they really know
what they're getting into?

I don't care, he had responded, the money is good—the
best. And pointing to the land surrounding them, he
added that to plant your feet on these soils was a luxury
few could afford. Living here was a privilege, and that yes,
some of the men needed the money to survive the cost of
city living, and that others were just motivated by greed
the same way black-flies seek comfort inside the creases of
your neck, but true living—the kind we see and breathe
in tandem with the bears that dawdle our dirt streets and
the caribou that run the icy rivers and the salmon that seek
to die where more life will be made—compels the soul
that wants to feel it. Only stupidity keeps these men from
seeing what I see. And for this suffering, I will never care.

Let's go, he tells her, they're waiting for us, and he grabs
her hand and leads her to the tail of the plane, avoiding
the four blades that have become a circle of fuzzy gray. Be
careful, he says as he feels the blades pushing and cutting
into the air. Hurry up. Once at the top of the ramp, he says,
walk to the front, our seats are there.

The cockpit?

Yes, my noble one, the cockpit.

Fort-Chimo, and the wind is pushing horizontal lines of snow in every direction. How on Earth could life possibly be worse than back home? she yells to her father as they disembark the plane.

This is the tundra, not the taiga, Adeline.

The difference being we will die if we stay more than an hour here, she quips. And to think this place once was called Fort Good Hope.

They run to the large Suburban waiting for them and slide into the front seats. He puts the car into drive. Did you know that Fort-Chimo, *saimuuq* to the Inuits, means 'Let's shake hands,' Adeline.

No, Dad, I did not. Let's shake hands? How about giving it the flip?

Adeline, stop it.

Sorry, it's just that—

And soon, Chimo will change its name again, to Kuujjuaq, The Great River.

Fabulous.

Adeline …

They leave the makeshift airport behind, and he turns the car onto the road leading to the village. Adeline tightens the furred hoody of her puffer right up to her chin and looks ahead through the windshield. She thinks about hope, its meaning here—a wishful thought. Why are we here exactly, Dad?

A meeting.

About?

Some engineer wants to talk environment with me.

He couldn't come to us?

I thought I'd make it a trip. With you. A side-glance and he takes her hand. You'll remember this one day, I know you will.

Sure Dad, when I'm somewhere lost in Abu Dhabi's desert looking for water inside a camel's hump.

He turns to her, eyes squinting, and his laugh—humor and complicity-filled, telling her levity is not so out of reach, not here, with him. Good luck with that one, he says. Not sure they have camels there, Adeline.

A smile forms on her face, and she looks at his profile. The hard hat tipping to the right, the cigarette tucked behind his ear—the one hanging off his mouth, the nose, crooked and flirting with its aquiline gene. It's nice to be with you, Dad. Thank you. She wiggles on her seat, scans the landscape before them, and asks, how come you know all this anyway?

I don't know. There is arrogance in his eyes, and he reminds her he is the youngest manager at the helm of the largest hydro project in America. A smile comes. I guess I picked it up. Easy thing, he shrugged.

The land, flat, is fierce in its power to expose and destroy, surrounding them. And the powder, these whippings of white, as if raging to push Adeline and John Brodeur toward a foreign fiefdom that has never belonged to their kind. We're almost there, he says, pointing to the few houses they could now see.

That's it?

That's it. But first, this.

He swerves the truck toward the water bordering the land. The drive is slow—silent for a while until she hears his whistling. They roll until they reach a wooden fence, high but thin.

The winds are picking up, he says, and he barters his hard hat for an orange and white tuque.

She smiles. Dad … You look funny with that on.

I do, do I? But not as weird looking as these dinosaurs, he laughs. You're all buttoned, right?

I am.

All right, then. Let's go.

They step out of the car and walk to the wooden enclave, the sound of crusted snow under their feet, buried by the noise of drafts. The animals, tall and large turn around for a moment toward the winds which keep veering, and with their qiviut lifted by the swirly air, they remain, immovable Goliaths from another time, oblivious to the elements.

She remains standing with her hands resting atop the fence and observes their horns, ornaments like foreheads made of wood matter. Some are smaller than others, she says.

The males have the larger ones.

Why am I not surprised.

Well, what can I tell you … Anyway, look. They are made for this place, Adeline. It's in their blood. They are majestic, aren't they?

She hears the words and her mother's face appears. Maybe that is why she is the way she is. Because she has no protection from the elements that have produced her. Something went amiss.

Between 1973 and 1978, last year, basically, Quebec released forty-two muskoxen, not quite mature ones, northwest of Fort-Chimo, just along the south shore of Ungava Bay. What you see here is part of the result. Their calves.

Adeline bringing her arms around her shoulders, looks on further, beyond the dozen large animals who know nothing else than what they were born for. And when you are happy, she thinks, you reproduce, project all you think you know about who or what you are onto this blank canvas that is not as blank as you think it is—

Dad, where to now? I'm cold ...

They hop back into the truck and follow the road leading back to the village for fifteen minutes. Reaching a blue trailer, a random-looking trailer lost in this enclave made of others, they park the Suburban and walk to the door. Thick ice has piled onto each of the stairs and as they climb to the entrance, Adeline holds on to her father's arms, his steadiness a usual cane.

Come in and wait for me here, Adeline, he says, pointing to the back of the trailer. His hands are in his pocket, searching. Twenty should be enough. He puts the two ten-dollar bills in her hand. His face has changed, his posture, too. It's as if a different wind was with them; with him mostly.

I have become invisible.

She grabs the money, looks around and understands they have entered inside the village's general store. Half-stocked shelves displaying non-perishable goods surround her, and to her right, near the entrance, there's an Inuit man standing behind the cash register, not really seeing her. Looking farther in, she sees where her father wants her to wait, a small bar adjacent to the store where a few men stand and drink. The smell of beer reaches her, and the Inuit man speaks words she cannot understand.

Give me two hours, her father says.

She watches him disappear behind a set of beaded curtains, watches the strings sway and clatter until they don't. She walks to the bar, chooses to sit at one of the two available tables, far from the counter. There are no windows. There is no view other than what is there—those men, drunk and absent from themselves, very much like this place. Where has Dad gone, she wonders, as she roots inside her backpack for her Walkman. A meeting here, in this shithole? Her headphones—a vice holding her skull, she feels something of a wave threaten to flood her gut. She presses on play, but the device remains idle—the batteries are empty. She keeps her headphones on, pretending she is away, pretending she is taming impatience; pretending she is content here in this place, cold, and just cold. She closes her eyes and falls asleep, asking herself where her father is—and why.

The sounds of more clattering and John Brodeur appears, a woman behind him clenching the back of his jacket. Whose leash is it, Adeline wonders, her eyes watered from the smoke-filled room. She checks her watch. It's been three hours, Dad. We're going to be late.

I know. The plane is waiting for us. I already warned Mom.

The bar is filled with more men and the sounds coming out of their mouths is like the smell of the beer they are drinking—profuse and stultifying.

Put your jacket on Adeline. We're leaving now.

Adeline slides her puffer jacket on, and observes her father and the woman that keeps following him with eyes inside which intimacy dances, still. Intimacy—this notion, a rumor now inside her home.

The woman is younger than her mother, much younger, Adeline can tell. And she thinks more, of her mother, breathing under this other sky, living and waiting in other snows and other colds. For them. For her husband.

The woman approaches her, and Adeline takes a step back, her heart beating too fast. Her father walks to her, kisses both her cheeks and tells the woman something about the agreement being fair, and that yes, if all goes according to plan, it would be possible. Adeline does not understand, she only knows they must leave, for her mother is marking time, hoping, most likely seated on the rocking chair that quiets her angst and frames more knowledge of what is unfolding not so distant from her, smoking her pipe and swaying.

John Brodeur takes Adeline by the waist, pulls her to the door, to the night—the revelation to come.

What was that all about, Dad? she asks, seated on the edge of her seat. *That* was your meeting?

Chimo doesn't have that many options for office meetings.

She's your *engineer*?

Brodeur nods as the truck reaches the airport.

Looking at him, she sees something she has never seen before, but she can't name the feeling; she can't define its meaning. Her breathing has become shallow. Why bring me at all, Dad?

Your mother and I, Adeline ... I don't know anymore.

Strawberry-like patches are surfacing, she feels, under her collarbone, hot redness that is spreading. You want my permission, Dad? What is it you want exactly? To tell you this woman is good for you—me?

I wanted you to see her.

Adeline sinks in her seat, head bent. Why on Earth?

John Brodeur brings a hand atop the hardhat placed to his right and taps his fingers to the rhythm of the new pounding inside his head.

You fooled me into thinking this trip was about us. It never was.

He points his chin to the windshield. The winds will die soon.

I don't know about that.

Adeline, I wanted you to see her so you would know, like a warning of things to come. A promise of something better, maybe, too.

Which is?

You know …

The tunnel of white—darkened by their speed. Mom, she whispers. And turning to him, she continues, telling him she never asked for any of this. Never asked for the burden of being his friend. You could have asked Coco, she lets out.

Come on. Your sister is not you.

No, she isn't. But she could share the burden. Not just me here. I deserve peace.

Stop it. Leave her out of this. You, you understand, and you are older.

And because I understand, it makes me worthy, of what exactly?

The man remains—what he is. Amorphous, adopting the shapes he knows, the ones he has worn and lived and practiced. Everything around them has become flat, even the air.

I pulled from life more than she can ever understand, your mother. I pulled all a net can pull. The good and the foul. The foul, however, she cannot manage.

What's the foul, Dad? What is it?

Success.

Success?

Success.

Chimo, your success? She chews the inside of her mouth, pauses, but she cannot tame her indignation. You can't abandon someone you love, she yells. You can't just leave them because they haven't turned out to be the way you thought they would. You used her. Her looks. Her poise. Mom is elegant, classy. Not like this other woman I just saw. And she's fat. Her eyes become larger, and she shakes her head, disbelief inside her brain. And you always tease Mom about her ass.

She's a teacher.

I don't care what she is, Dad. Never will. Mark my words. She's just a vulgar woman leeching on to a married man. If that is not vulgar, I don't know what is.

The airport appears, its lights few, sparse, and the Hercules is waiting. The car, he parks 100 meters from the aircraft and in silence they step out, and they walk. The engines are roaring and as they enter from the back of the plane, she knows the drill; knows to walk straight to the cockpit, sit and fasten her seatbelt on the jump seat closest to the pilot.

Home, she tells them.

We know, young lady, they reply, amused.

Right.

The flight is smooth, and the engine's rumble is filling a space that would otherwise be empty. The pilots laugh—at what? She cannot tell and Brodeur doesn't care. He has fallen asleep, assuaged by the plane's tremors, its song efficient because steady, continuous.

The plane's wheels hit the frozen tarmac and awakens Brodeur. It doesn't startle Adeline. They wait for the plane to still, look at the ramp slowly unfolding, feel the wind lash at their faces, biting, and unbuckle.

Let's go, he tells her.

They walk to the truck parked near the airport's porch and as they do, they hear the plane's engine slowly fading. Adeline slides in the front while her father unplugs the heat cord from the front end of the truck.

What will you tell her? Adeline asks.

That the meeting took longer.

You are killing her with deception.

If she wanted different, she would change.

You know she can't! She's sick!

Adeline thinks of her mother's incapacity to transform, adapt. She knows Eva Brodeur's goal is not to be light—easy. Her mother's beliefs are simple, yet archaic: The more a female barks and hisses and spits, the more epidermal the reaction, the deeper the validation.

She looks at him. The silence is short. She knows, Dad. She might be crazy, but she *is* a woman.

I don't know that she does. Know.

Of course, you think that. The truth, and you know it—she is not getting better.

I know, she's not ...

Then why do this, Dad? To her. And to me ... stop thinking I'm part of this.

Adeline, stop ...

I'm sure you've thought of doing what that man did, Dad, she seethes.

Brodeur's eyes narrow. His jaw tightens. The car swerves, as the tires skid, floating above the ice. Brodeur pumps the brakes, steadies the direction. Okay, he says. The road is sinuous, and there are no other cars meeting them, nothing telling them a world exists beyond the place they are seeing. Brodeur pulls the cigarette nestled behind his ear, pushes the car lighter, and as he does, movement, more life than shadow, and it pulls their sight to the side of the road.

What was that?

Brodeur, exhales, says he doesn't know.

Another movement stains the road, and he presses on the brakes.

Michi! she yells out.

The dog has frozen in a defying stance and is looking at them beyond the truck's lights. At her chest, the usual blond and white of her coat are now partially colored. From her mouth, a willow, soft and disarticulated, is hanging.

She escaped again. I'm going to get her, Adeline says as she quickly opens the door.

She walks slowly and the dog wags its tail but clenches the pheasant's neck more. As Adeline approaches, the dog takes a few steps back, her hind legs leading, both father and daughter watching her assessing what to do—retreat into her instincts. Adeline whispers, come Michi, you dumb dog, get in the damn truck. Now. The dog knows the tone and darts into the forest, its loot rocking inside a locked grip.

Adeline stays in the middle of the road, her back is to the truck, the truck's high beams marking obscurity. She turns around, faces what she cannot see, but knows he is there, looking at her. He flicks on the beams, and she walks back to the car, this time sliding in the back seat.

We're turning around, Adeline. They just called me. Over the radio.

Who did?

Dam security.

What happened?

Your mother, that's what happened.

When they roll in, security's beige truck is parked at the end of the road, ten meters from the KA3 dam, aside Eva Brodeur's sedan. The truck's revolving lights are idle, casting none of its intermittent red-lighting on anything. Or anyone.

From where she sits, Adeline scans the scene before her—a white fairyland soon to become dystopian. And in tandem their eyes canvass the air. In tandem they look and see. The same pain.

Projectors angled along the dam are lighting the shroud of snow surging from gun-like machines positioned twenty meters from the dam. Snow cannons, her father says, their sole purpose is to isolate the dams' core from the frost.

I don't care for your civil engineering lessons, Dad. And I know all of that, anyways.

Artificial snow knitted for dams, she thinks—a white and powdery quilt onto which a silhouette is seen staggering. Mom, she says, opening the passenger door. Mom.

Brodeur steps from the car, running to one of the agents in charge of dam surveillance. How long has she been standing here?

The men stare at each other, the noise of engine hovering over them. We've been here for over an hour, sir, the man yells out. I don't know. From what we saw just before you got here, the cold is just starting to set in. -40 C. The blood is like slush ...

Blood?

The man nods. We tried, Mr. Brodeur, to pull her off—the third time this winter—but the more we tried, the worse she became. She got physical. Called you immediately. We're waiting for the ambulance to arrive. They told us forty-five minutes. That was an hour ago.

And Brodeur thinks of the Meo River. Of the secrets it still holds—answers the man he had not saved had chosen to pursue. He thinks of Adeline's words, too, inhales all slowly.

The winds suddenly intensify, cutting into the snow the cannons jet into the air. Flurries land on their faces, soft lashes of cold that run like pearls along their cheeks. Adeline dries some of it from her face, eyes detailing the contours of Eva Brodeur's body. Let me go to her, she says, frantic, she always listens to me. She did last time. As she implores, with her eyes, her hands, too, movement coming from the edge of the forest catches their attention. Michi, the girl yells, her breath dancing before her. She turns to her father. I'm going, Dad. If you go, you'll only make it worse. You always do, she seethes, her breath carving into the air. You've always been a trigger. Always.

Michi has reached her mistress, wagging her tail, waiting for Eva to move, and barking, too. Eva is swaying with her back against the harsh lighting of men, blinded by her thoughts, razor-dulled, her coat wrapped around her shoulders, a fury of wolf fur covering the sparkling blue of the turtleneck that is still clinging to her—and she stands, unresponsive, a cadence booming into their ears. Adeline hears Eva's voice—words surging from a large, dry, and fleshy lips, red and blood-stained—the undecipherable syllables on repeat, soft and hitting a same key; a same note.

A catatonic state.

Mom, Adeline says, as she takes her by the shoulders, startled by the depth of the fur, she wants to shake her mother. Instead, she turns Eva's face toward her own, waves her hand in front of her mother's eyes, wanting to summon a response. The woman's gray eyes have darkened and her lips, ruby red, are wounded by what can only be relentless biting. From the pulped flesh, blood keeps coming, pure and resisting the cold. Eva raises her finger and pokes at the condensation and swirls it around, the breathing etching the space they share. Looking at her daughter, she slowly brings her hands farther up, to the side of her head, and without a sound, pulls both the gold loops down from her ears, slicing the lobes—perfect trickles of blood. Adeline takes a step back. The usual is staring back at her, mushy and soft. What would she be thinking if she really looked at me, she wonders. Is there mushiness there, too, on my face? My body? Like the mushiness that lives inside of her—it's like you want me to make sure I will never surface, she tells her, like you. Grow. Confusion is sneaking into Adeline's mind, a fog, thick and infertile. How original, she thinks—beauty never beats insanity. Insanity always wins, dismisses. A dame's core, unblanketed. Exposed. My mother.

She takes her hand, holding it tightly. And the mother follows the daughter, follows the markings of a child that never was one. Adeline feels the poundage of eyes latching on to her shoulders, this anchor that should be weighed. Stopping at the end of the dam, John Brodeur is staring at them both. Adeline turns around, lifting her mother's face to hers'. This time, you're leaving Mom. We're medevacking you out of here, tonight. Forever. Come Michi, she continues. And stop licking the blood off her hands.

The truck slowly rolls onto the driveway and Brodeur immobilizes the car and cuts the engine. The time is 6:00 a.m.

They look up. To the entrance door, open, its base stuck to the snow that has accumulated on the porch. Dense. Hard.

They step from the Suburban, Michi jumping out first, alert and eager. Swatting the snowflakes away, Brodeur plugs in the truck's block heater as Adeline retrieves the yard leash stretched along the side of the house. She picks it up and sees the swivel snap is broken. She climbs the outdoor staircase, dragging the dog cable along. Dumb dog, she says again, grabbing her collar and walking into the house. Come on girl, go in.

Her breath is visible—more clouds coming into her home. Eva's new signature, unavoidable, meets her sight: four candles almost dead but still burning, and a coulis of red wax pooled at the base of the chamber-sticks. On a white and lacy tablecloth. Is it really wax? she asks herself.

The round table has been set for three. The plates, porcelain and gold rimmed at the edge, are empty. Between the candles, a chicken roast stands, surrounded by some other dishes Adeline cannot make out. A full bottle of wine, too, is waiting beside a plate where a lemon meringue pie has been set. Dad's favorite, she knows. Tears come to her eyes. Hadn't Dad said not to expect us for dinner?

Both Adeline and her father look at the spread now exposed by the amber of the ceiling lamp. Adeline bends over the table, touches the food one dish at a time, poking a finger into them. All so cold, she whispers. She looks at her father. A cold chaos, that's us.

Pineapple Diet

I MET YOU INSIDE the small school located ten minutes by foot from our village. Grade seven, French class, is where it happened. Our desks side-by-side, we started to talk, an easy yet hesitant talk, assessing signs of commonalities, even the ragged-edged ones. You had come from Montreal's south shore, a suburbanite incognizant of the soil's rules. But even if you had known them—to learn to fold onto yourself until the sun went down, it would have made no difference. Nothing ever fazed you, something I long mistook for strength. Nervously playing with my bangs and pulling a strand of hair to my mouth, I explained where I had moved from—another camp south to the one we now lived in—and that during those three previous years, I had attended an English-speaking school, but had been tutored by a French teacher, a neighbor, to keep up with my French school level. My mom's idea. You nodded, looking at me, impassivity in your gaze—you were always so misleading, your body language a mismatch to your soothing words. About this teacher, the source of the day's demise, if you recall me sharing at recess—Gisele was her name, I mostly remember her hand, her right hand, its deformity. A rump; a thalidomide casualty, and when, during the first private class, she had secured her large, black-rimmed glasses up the bridge of her nose with this grotesque-looking ball of skin and bone, I did what no child my age would have done: I simply smiled.

Every Saturday morning for three years, I walked the few meters to her house, eager to leave my home. A better place to be me, soon to be reached, I hoped. From those moments when leaving my house, I remember the snow-banks towering over the borough we lived in. I remember dragging my hand across Michi's coat and thinking about nothing. Not questioning the precocity of a growing void. Single houses, they were called, ours was a double, like yours, allotted only to those holding management posi-tions, childless or not. The French lessons should have lasted an hour, but they never did, extending into the realms of her private life. Smiling, tweaking her short, curly hair, and placing it nervously behind her ears, she'd prepared for me her signature maple syrup-laced tapioca pudding, talking non-stop, a stream of unconsciousness, fascinating as much as disturbing—I became her unlikely confidante on the sad subject of childlessness, stranger yet, an expert on matters related to colon health. And so, from ages nine to twelve, while trying to polish and refine my mother's tongue, I learned about life's humors: the plight of being motherless; about agony, death's leech; about fibre; about the importance of drinking water, its loosening power.

The impact on my French lessons was watered-down, too. She had been a distraction for me, as I had been for her. A child to hold, to get lost into. An adult woman in want of me. It felt good. Sane.

This time, with her, unorthodox as much as strange, wove a path, certain, inevitable; to when the world would finally discover the truth about my knowledge of the French language.

That first day, I cried in front of the whole class—seven students, I know, it isn't much, but still, they were boys. Grammar, my said forte. Hadn't Gisele said so? I had failed the quiz, and miserably so. My first devastating encounter with humiliation. I was in shock, unable to understand where I had fumbled—reflexive verbs, reciprocal verbs, the damn past participles? And, of course, the four-foot tall, bug-eyed nun would remind me of this fact until the end of the school year.

The dancing, the intelligence behind your mischievous smile, Charlotte. Have a honey drop, you said, placing the candy in my hand. No calories in there, you winked.

Inside these wooden parts, a hesitant bond held us, and we let it. It was a year of magical unfolding, that year, no? Our burgeoning obsession for thinness welding you to me—me, to you. We knew nothing of Karen Carpenter's similar quest, or that of so many others', the recognition of eating disorders emerging slowly elsewhere around the western world except where we lived. I've asked myself, maybe you have, too, how was it that, away from civilization's pressures on the woman's body, social media a sci-ence-fictive abstraction, abstinence's highs so easily lured us?

The want for control knows no limits; no boundaries, and I think to myself as I write this, it can, and will, unfold its root inside the jungle's soil as much as the taiga's per-mafrost.

It doesn't need a passport to its own cold hell.

Our time together came to an end: June 1978.

We both had nurtured the same crush, you must remember, admit—if not, this is your coming out, too—fantasizing over the camp's doctor, our parents' good friend, twenty-seven-year-old, Dr. Bartolucci.

The Italian kamikaze.

The evening came, full of daylight, an evening we knew would come, our parents organizing a dinner party to celebrate our admission to our respective boarding schools. The local school, the only one, did not offer classes beyond the seventh grade. You, of course, would attend a French-speaking establishment, a posh girl's school located in the city, while my parents, my mother, really, had decided to quench her thirst to be seen, by money, by jewelry—the English breed—through me, and were sending me, against my will, to an English-speaking boarding school located in Quebec's Eastern Townships. French had become a nuisance to her status. Schizophrenia of the tongue, I still call it. At least, I remember thinking, while moving into my dorm later that year, the British-like den was a co-ed one.

It took us one week to devise our summer plans.

In your bedroom that evening, animated by our mission's promise of teenage fun, to the sound of our parents laughing and drinking, we typed our grail on your colored 1970 Olympia Traveller Deluxe, finalizing our vacation itinerary: Montreal, Provincetown, Massachusetts, missing sand and beach and the pull of feeling lost inside buoyant crowds, we would stop along the way, visiting the likes of Burlington, Manchester-by-the-Sea, Norwich.

Only thirteen years old—a very sad affair—we needed a chaperone.

Dark and stormy Lucca Bartolucci was our choice.

I remember the walk through the corridor leading to the dining room, project in hand, and taking a seat at the dining table. We refused more of the food—a funky casserole made of fish the men had caught that day; the sherbet your mom had filled inside a hollowed orange, too. It was you who interrupted the conversation, your hand swaying in everyone's faces, quieting them to attention, too. It was you who spoke, and I was happy it wasn't me.

Of course, what were we thinking? They all said, no.

The funny part was no one laughed, the paradox etching a smile only onto Bartolucci's boyish face.

Back in your bedroom, feeling let down, we slid into our nightgowns. We hadn't eaten for two days, and hunger, this unavoidable stalker, was tugging at both our stomachs. Remember my teacher? I asked you. Fibre-made Gisele. The laughter was sudden, deep, and for a moment, at the thought of her, we became one again. Pineapples, I told you, your mom has a pyramid of pineapple Del Monte cans mounted in her pantry. I saw it open. They were looking at me.

Your eyes spoke to me, as I explained the miracle behind the binge-eating of pineapple. This miracle food, as much as we want, I insisted. And we'll never gain weight again. That's what they said, the doctors. That's what Gisele had told me.

I remember vividly, the empty cans stashed on your desk, the lids littering the floor, our fingers twirling slice after slice of sticky, yellow-fleshed fruit into the air. The acid reflux about to flood our throats, the soft tissues inside of our mouths waiting to be blistered.

We tended to this friendship as much as we could, as much as we knew how, but eventually, like so many ill-kept things in life do, we drifted, even in spite of that one last time. An improvised farewell.

The other night, I searched for your face on the Internet and stumbled upon two pictures of you. I smiled at the first one: an old wedding photo of you and the wealthy owner of an American engineering firm. The football player you had talked to me about that one time, I thought, for sure. The article mentioned you studied philosophy. McGill University. Then, this other one, a more recent one, an academic text signed by you—the philosophy of aesthetics and the luxury industry, a novel understanding—accompanied by an over-saturated, full-body photograph of the author. You.

I leaned closer to the screen, and zooming in, I scrutinized your face.

You have barely changed, Charlotte.

The smile, equivocal.

The dirty-blonde hair.

The eyes, double hooks.

And you still live there, I read. A philosopher of the cold.

And a body just as thin. Like mine.

Omnipotence

Saturday night at the Red Caribou Lounge, the only bar inside the camp, the place Pam Knox calls her weekend home. And tonight, the small crowd is a good one, febrility-filled.

She stands in the entrance, feet on its threshold—a bouncer like a black-haired goddess. Yet her face, apish-looking, displays a young mouth already quoted by deep lines, a philtrum too long, under which thin straight lips, should bore any looker. The only ascendance she will ever hold, over men, women, too, comes from her puppy-shaped eyes. Clear-blue and wide, bending to the ground like lost arrows, her eyes command, endear, even. The men fall for her, she knows, at the club. Like insects hungry for pollen—emotionally deficient men, seduced by her apparent air of mystery—suicidal distress she has trained her eyes to hide, unable to detect foul from fragrant. They don't know she is lukewarm at best—a deliquesced being. And when the main door swings back and forth, a line of men standing and hoping, appear to her—about twenty of them. She looks on, the power of condescension moving her eyes, the scent coming to her, a cloud of cheap alcohol-filled sweetness carried by the freeze-dried air. To her and to all the other girls dancing behind her, on a floor, baby powdered and wet with sweat.

They are anxious, these men. They know the odds are against them—the camp is home to 1,000 men and fifty women—that having cleaned and shaved and traded their workers' uniforms for the only evening attire they have brought from home doesn't guarantee their entry into the women-run club.

Everyone is waiting for something, she thinks. I did. Let *them*, too.

Hey Pam, she hears, let me in, come on, I'll give you a twenty.

The currency around here is a woman, she yells out to him from the porch. You know that, Henry. Cross yourself a little more, she laughs, knees in the snow, maybe then, you'll get chosen. The unchosen one, most of you, she whispers.

And while the men laugh at Henry, whose eyes shrink into slitted holes, beaded by humiliation, they also know they are laughing at themselves—giant men working this land made of warrior waters.

One woman, two men, Henry. That's the rule. The mule rule, she seethes.

Now, she thinks, be obedient.

A tall girl approaches from the back of the line, a beautiful blonde, alone and not looking like she plans to be, for long. The men still for a moment, their banter halted by hope, and their breath draws into the wall that is the cold, the only movement the night will offer—hunger that will need to be tamed. Somehow. She dawdles along the line of men, holding her fur coat tightly around her waist, scrutinizing the men, one at a time.

Holly, Pam yells from the open door, a pad and pen in hand, two more. After that, no more entries, honey. The club is maxed out.

Holly nods, walking back and forth, a zigzag along the queue, until she sees one man she could examine; maybe want. She stops. What's your name?

Damian, *Holly.*

Ah. *Damian.* Nice name. Looking at him more, she takes his hand, another man's hand randomly, too. Flanked by her Saturday night captures, she climbs the stairs to the club. At the door, she remains, watching her escorts cross into her territory, watching them walk to the bar as they contemplate the crowd of women moving to the rhythms of the moment, voltage striking at her mind.

Before entering, she turns toward the line of men, and smiles. They are still waiting, hoping—unaware. Unaware that behind them, 200 meters from where they stand, a female polar bear quietly sits, her coat impeccably white, a fluffy, round cub by her side. The month of May, she thinks, sticking her tongue out to capture the snowflakes the wind pushes into her mouth, should be fertile.

And after she blows them a kiss, a gesture soaked in theatrical mockery, the tall blonde turns back to step into the club. Pam, she yells, feeling warmth reaching her gait. Time to lock the door.

Donuts and
Coffee

My mother is pacing in the kitchen, whispering to herself—maybe to me as well? I don't care to decipher her mumblings and look at my watch. 10:30 a.m. They will be here soon.

She tells me to make the coffee, and I grab the drip coffee maker from inside the cupboards, placing it on the counter, fitting its conical shape with a number two Melitta filter.

For twelve cups, she reminds me, as she takes a cigarette from her pack and lights her Cameo stick.

Yes, Mom, twelve.

The coffee tin is empty, and so I take the can opener and remove the lid from a new one. I feel the cold scent of coffee lifting to my face, seeping into my nostrils. I close my eyes, and I think of why I am here, back in Montreal, taking care of this adult bullshit I know too much about.

I slowly fill the reservoir with water, watching it rise one level at a time until it reaches the number twelve mark. I remain still, play with my hair, and hope none of my mother's operatic airs will burst into my ears. Histrionic-filled music, so she thinks, soothes her nerves. I beg to differ.

I know I did the right thing, that I really didn't have a choice, someone had to tell her the truth. And I think of my father, curse him. The rock star of the civil engineering world, yes, tall and handsome, and witty, loved by most, respected by all.

Yet the man is so very flawed.

It's time to open the box, she tells me, and you forgot to plug the coffee. I'll do it.

Her voice startles me. I turn to her, so close, still, to the past I am recalling, and certain more of the same will always be there, waiting for me, at every corner of my life with her—them. She is thin and short, her body half-bent, cannot straighten, enduring the consequences of a botched tummy tuck that almost killed her. Fat necrosis, the doctors said, and she should have stopped smoking. Her face is scary-done, filled with harsh rouge high above her cheekbones and bright purple markings over her eyelids. I look at her lips, plump and chapped. I smell the cigarette-breath escaping her mouth.

Her face wears the color living inside her moment, I think, the color inside decent and perfect bruising. I don't understand what it is I feel for her. All I know is being away from her has always made sense. It puzzles me. Why am I doing this for her? Do I have an ulterior motive?

She hands me a large oval plate and I set it on the table.

All, she tells me.

All? We're only four, Mom. There's sixteen.

All.

I place the glazed donuts on the edge of the serving plate and fill the middle with the sprinkled and Boston cream ones. The arrangement is tentative, but I don't really care.

I lick the sugar off my fingers as we both lean against the oak kitchen table and wait. I hear her breathing. I hear the smacking of her lips. I know dryness is taking hold of her mouth, matching the rest of what is inside her, I think. It would explain much of this uneasiness I carry with me when with her.

We hear a car park in the driveway. She puts her cigarette out in the sink and throws it in the garbage bin.

You answer, she tells me.

Of course, I tell myself, you are a coward, too.

Walking to the portico, I bring the strap of my overalls back to the top of my shoulder and think I should not have told her anything. He shouldn't have confided in me, making me his accomplice, making me validate his decision.

Your mom and I, you know, he had said.

I know, Dad. Remember.

And it's true, I did understand, too. Between them, only the obligation to pretend. And now the obligation was dying a most natural death.

She's going back to Montreal, she's fixing up the house we just bought, he told me on the phone at the end of my school year. You, you stay with me for the summer. I got you a job. Pays real well, like usual. Secretarial work.

I went, took the plane ride up north, stayed in the house that had been my family's for ten years—a brown and beige prefabricated house nestled at the end of a tree-filled cul-de-sac.

Inside that house, waiting for me, as if my father had orchestrated all its display, my mother's closet—inside the closet, new styles, none of them hers. *The famous engineer's.*

For two months, I worked and lived in the taiga I came to tame so well, never probing, simply observing. I think I decided not to care a long time ago. Too much to care about can halt a heart. Detachment comes easy to a young woman like me. Or is it dissociation?

I hear the water filter the coffee, knowing it's almost done, the sound of it percolating through the air, and I feel as though brown drips of time fall onto themselves inside the pot. My life measured like this.

I wait more, my back against the wall, near the entrance, and recall: the end of my summer work, a warm day, my mother picking me up at the airport. All of it is so vivid, morbidly so. She drove us back to the home that was broken, and watching her gripping the steering wheel, I had seen a different apathy in her eyes.

How are things over there? she asked.

You must know, I risked.

What is it I should know?

I had just finished reading a history book on ancient warfare—messengers were as hated as the message they carried. My mother would never forgive me for telling the truth. I had wished for my father to be transparent with her, if only to protect me, from the violence beating inside her instability. No. Passive passiveness more than passive aggression defines my father. Conflict avoiders have no balls, I think, and wonder, more: How was he ever able to conceive me with no balls? Am I miracle? To this I say, yes, that I am. Two cowards producing decency must be qualified as a miracle.

Yes, there is another woman, I blurted out, as we turned onto our street. You know her... she moved to camp, then to our house, became Coco's teacher ...

And there it was, a courage that had morphed into stupidity.

The silence smelled of ambivalent resentment, and once parked in the driveway, she ran to the house, with me in tow. Scared, I saw her pick up the receiver, saw the rotary dial turn and turn. Sunday, dinnertime, and she was calling my father's big boss, and the words flowing from her throat were deafening.

Yes, I had seen the conclusion, firmly forgone. Call it adolescence's early-onset wisdom, a mental illness yet to be discovered and named.

My mother would eventually understand she wouldn't be returning. To her husband. To me. To a land she had grown to love.

And maybe I, too, will never see any of my land again—become cold-drunk, again.

Here, now, the doorbell is ringing, and I walk toward the door. I see them through the glazing.

Hi, I say, pulling the door in.

They smile back, but barely. I focus on him, forgetting about his wife. Tall and large, a former quarterback, he is wearing an all-brown suit, and his hair, what is left of it is limping at the front of his head with curly and whispery bangs. He looks like a giant Hershey Kiss, I think to myself.

Come inside please, she is waiting.

They slowly walk into the living room, choose to sit on two separate swivel chairs, my mother electing to sit at the start of the L-shaped sofa, close to them.

She motions her finger through the air, telling me to do what I am supposed to do.

I go to the kitchen, fill the silver tray with a creamer, a sugar bowl, three spoons, three cups, three saucers, and a stack of napkins.

When I return to the living room, the woman and my mother are crying.

I know, she tells my mother, so terrible, her eyes turning to her husband.

The man looks at me. I can see it in his eyes, he doesn't want to be here.

I can't help but smile.

Let me get the donuts, I hear myself say, that and the coffee.

I come back, place the items on the coffee table, and as I do, I hear my mother plead for this man to find my father a new job, to relocate him—Saudi Arabia, Brazil, maybe—away from this other woman.

His wife says, yes, that it could help, don't you think, honey? Saudi Arabia is the best, there, the women are covered.

Wonderful idea, I whisper, shaking my head. As if?

An expression of powerlessness deforms his face.

The woman sips her coffee, places the cup back on the saucer perched on her lap, and proceeds to add more sugar and cream to it.

Why he has chosen this short, fat woman, over you, I do not know.

My mother shakes her head, the disbelief painful, her humiliation murdering a faltering ego.

He always told me I was big, you know, called me a big ass. Her hand caresses the sofa's fabric. But can't we all agree, this woman has a bigger one than mine.

I pinch myself. She can't be talking about this. But she is, and as much as I dread staying, a part of me recognizes the humor living inside the moment's absurdity. Just a few more minutes, I promise myself. Then I leave.

From under the sofa cushion, she pulls out the latest edition of the faraway-town's local newspaper. She finds the page and points to the picture of a woman standing by a river, fishing rod in hand. Only her backside is shown and yes, it is large, filled with dents planted by a bad case of cellulite gone mad. I am thinking that yes, for a picture to betray this much …

I turn to the man, who is looking straight ahead, sipping his coffee.

But you've lost so much weight, the woman adds, tapping the side of her thigh. She smiles an unconvincing smile. Your derrière is more than fine.

And it continues, and I smile a convincing one.

Images mingle inside my head, of my mother walking topless on St-Barth's beaches years before, of how nothing looked as if it would hold, her breasts as much as her tush. And of this past summer when walking into my parent's bedroom, and how I found his mistress naked, standing with a towel wrapped around her head. Evidently, both of their asses seemed to be filled with jelly of the expired kind. And why had Mother not chosen to have her ass lifted, anyway?

The crying brings me back. The sobbing is loud and the mucus abundant.

I give my mother a tissue and think of my evening plans. A concert. Genesis.

The man stays seated at the edge of the chair and is still holding the saucer in one hand and the cup in the other. All of him seems as if he were made of wax. I am not sure, but I think I hear some shaking, the spoon maybe clinking against the saucer? Or is it the cup tickling the saucer? Will he make it, I wonder, and what does his voice even sound like?

I smile at him again and decide to sit at the other extremity of the large L-shaped sofa, far from my mother. The vista is better.

The woman, dressed in a check-patterned dress reminiscent of a picnic tablecloth, has resumed her crying. She brings a tissue to her nose.

I look at the spread of donuts and pick the serving plate up. I walk to her. Take one please.

She quickly places her tissue inside her cleavage and becomes quiet. I can see she is hesitating between the maple and honey glaze confection.

I stare at her hand floating above the plate and try to understand the weight of her decision on my moment. My mother's moment. I see her jaw move from left to right. I see the concentration the moment requires.

She opts for the sprinkled variety.

You could have chosen better, I think.

When I turn to him, I see more panic has settled in his eyes. A donut?

His hand, now stable, like hers, hovers over the plate.

The Boston cream is quite good, I tell him as I put one on a napkin and place it in his hand. Have it.

He nods and takes a bite while I return to my seat. His eyes seem to thank me, I think.

From my back pocket I remove a pack of cigarettes and tap one out.

The man and the woman both swing the chairs, front to back. I see her wanting to grab another donut—a Boston cream maybe this time?

So good, she tells her husband. She hesitates.

The maple glaze never disappoint, I say after lighting up. Have one, you'll see.

She picks one up and starts to nibble at it.

My mother has become motionless. Her hands hold her kneecaps and her mouth is hanging half-open. I look at my watch and see they've been here for forty minutes, it's 11:30 a.m. All right, I think to myself. And my eyes speak a truth too old for a young girl such as me, to know. Feel. And I think, understand, the time to go is now, that there is nothing more to see or do here. Because this train wreck is mine, not yours, and that's all I got going for the moment.

He unfolds, does up his top button and brushes his hand across his hair. I notice the sweat pearling. I smile. We must be going, he says.

I walk to the woman. She is standing, brushing crumbs off her dress, and leaving them to fall on the carpet.

I'm sorry, she says.

Yes, Madame, so am I.

From the living room window, I watch her walk behind her husband. He opens the passenger door, and she slides onto the car seat.

When he reaches his side of the car, he lifts his head and looks at me looking at him.

He waves at me and when he does, I turn away from the window, leaving the curtains to sway.

Come here, I hear, make me more coffee.

As I do, the sound of Wagner fills the house—an operatic cacophony.

I pour her and I a large cup of coffee, bite into the last Boston cream, and I cannot help feeling the lack of melody inside this house now—the indulgence of sounds that cannot heal, hardcore and unforgiving. My mother now gone for good. Again.

I have to go, I tell her, picking my backpack from the floor. And while she says nothing, a drugged-out mouse, I know I must leave, as today is her birthday, and I have my own concert to attend.

Sail away, away, I sing to her, stepping out onto the cement porch. The sun is fully out. The sky, a sick blue. Be the true ripple that I need you to be, I think to myself, and never come back.

Duchess of Galina

SHE STANDS AT THE cafeteria entrance and knows she is seeing them for the last time.

It won't be enough, though.

A hesitation settles at the back of her throat, her hands damp, her skin tingling, and she wants to exhale the sight of these men. For so long now, she has done this, sixty days of strutting like a model on a runway made of stained, sticky linoleum.

The neon tubes hanging from the ceiling, fifty of them, highlight what she doesn't want the world to see.

Curves made of juvenile flesh.

The loudness dizzies her gait as she moves toward the food trays. She hears their voices—a choir composed of baritones and tenors synchronizing to her movement. She continues to walk the one hundred meters that separates her from the tray stacks.

It feels like an eternity.

She fights the urge to look up, to meet their faces, and she wishes she had the courage. She could reciprocate, pretend she doesn't care. But flattery is there, mixed with her timidity, weaving itself into the ambiguity these moments push her into—a fear that never leaves. She feels guilty, and she feels conflicted, this wanting to be seen; wanting attention. A beam that makes her feel good.

It scares her, and it's the last thing she will remember to never forget. The voices dimming—an abnormality. The silence broken by the swishing sound of a spoon sliding to the floor. A baby spoon, a bit like me, she would acknowledge years later, not smiling. The feeling of the spoon touching her heel before ricocheting on the steel leg of a table, spinning onto itself until reaching the far end of the industrial kitchen.

The laughter.

The flushing of a young face.

Adeline, feeling groggy, walks into the plane and looks around. What's going on guys, why's the Twin empty? Her voice, always calm, has a soprano hint to it. Hey there, the pilot says, headgear resting on his shoulders, we were expecting you to be on last night's flight. What happened? And yes, mornings aren't so popular around here, especially not on a Saturday.

My contract is done. Going back to the main camp before heading to Montreal in a couple of days.

Had a party, I see, the co-pilot says, brushing a finger under both his eyes.

She answers with a laugh, a noncommittal one, and one that says there is nothing to add, that it's none of your business, and scans the two rows of seats, choosing one close to the cockpit. That's it, guys, she says, last trip from this place.

You'll miss us.

Not so sure of that.

Not coming back next year?

You think the camp will still be here? It's a satellite camp. A sub-camp. But no, even if Dad insists, I am not coming back. Two hundred working men, ten women, eight out of which are over forty. No thank you.

They prepare the flight deck, switch what needs to be switched, and press what needs to be pressed. Well, whatever the case, you, Miss Adeline, are ours for the duration of this flight. Strap your seatbelt on because we are flying you through these skies, one last time—maybe?

And she thinks—hopes?—these men are good men, happy men, even, as if tied to a bond, to a higher order, taller and wider than the one their instincts could drive them to reach. Below. Flashes of the night before glide inside her belly. She swallows. Maybe the skies are where it's at? A place where you can hide and be more, where you fear nothing, and the horizon is beyond the keeping of dreams and hopes, because their weight is ignorant of all of life's tenses.

Safety.

She places her backpack on the seat beside hers. Something of a commotion bubbles inside her belly, collisions where emotions have become tactile. Lifting her head she watches the pilots maneuver, hears them speak with someone she assumes is guiding them from the pseudo control tower, and she sinks further into her seat, knowing the execution of her ritual is near.

Wait for the Twin to taxi to the bottom of the strip, she tells herself.

She looks through the porthole, and something in the skies is making her uneasy. The pearl-colored clouds are low, and she can feel the winds tugging at the fuselage. She blinks the unease away, takes a deep breath, listens to the engines revving up and she feels the small plane moving, the land there, and always so bare, always, and she thinks she hears it say it will never be more than what it is, that it doesn't care, because what the other worlds see as inclemency is exactly what it is, a violent core, one there to stay, no matter the destruction, no matter what humans will manage to extort from it.

Good-bye, Fontanges, she whispers to the camp, and see you never again.

The Twin Otter finally reaches the edge of the short runway, veers right, and comes to a semi-halt. The roar of the plane grows louder and its speed increases and she feels the small of her back being pushed against her seat, the only good sensation flying has ever given her.

When she feels the wheels conclude their barter with the ground—oil for air, ruggedness for levity, leaving the tarmac and becoming airborne, she starts to count from two hundred, backwards, until she thinks she is safe, unaware of the falsity inside her, that the world is flawed, and keeps pretending it's not.

We've reached cruising altitude, Adeline, she hears one of the two men yell. Should be there within the hour. Relax, honey. All will be okay.

Because they know her, she thinks, gratefully. Thanks guys. She wiggles her shoulders, retrieves a yellow Walkman from her backpack, presses play, and adjusts the headphones to her ears. Bowie.

Now, about last night.

She *thinks* she needs to recall it better.

She had packed a small suitcase, quickly gathering the few pieces of clothing she had brought with her for her week-to-week stays.

She had slid into her usual Lois jeans and oversized sweatshirt on which James Bay is written—bold and solid lettering, an ambivalence, about this place; this land, an unsustainable home at best.

Then, of course, her Kodiak boots, half-laced.

Charlotte, the only other girl still inside her trailer, had organized a farewell party. For you and me, Adeline. I'm leaving next week, too, remember?

Adeline had said, yes, she would go, and postpone her departure to the morning, not wanting to displease her friend. But in truth, she hadn't felt like attending the gathering, wishing instead to get back to the main camp and from there, return to the city as soon as possible. She felt out of place, just as any nineteen-year-old girl would.

Trailer number eight, the surveyors' lodging, and they had walked into room five, a bedroom soon to be stuffed with smoke and music. There had been gin and rum and mixes of some sort, the loudness filling the wanting of escaping this place.

Because time prolonged here was unforgiving.

Like all sleeping quarters laid out in each of the mobile homes, the room was deep but narrow. The crowd, typical of any Friday night in the wilderness, was boisterous. So much drunkenness, and so early for that, Adeline had thought.

Feeling as though already gone herself, she had chosen to remain close to the door while sipping a can of Coke.

His usual strut, holding a beer, she saw him walk toward her. His smile, bright, his eyes, welcoming. Off tomorrow, Adeline? the blond-haired surveyor had asked.

She fixed her hair. Jim, hey, yes. How about you, when are you going back to school?

In two weeks. This gig here was part internship, part not enough pleasure. Finishing your last year before graduation, I think?

Yes, and I can't wait.

He had remained standing, erect, like she was, to her left, and with intermittent side-looks had probed more. Tell me, what is it you missed most from life back home?

She had smiled before replying, considering the young man before her. It's lights, I suppose, and the sight of bright colored grass and the feeling of sunburn on my shoulders. I've fantasized about those everyday while hitting on the typewriter. True story.

And what's the first thing you're going to do when you get home?

A movie, then Dairy Queen, she had laughed.

"Risky Business?"

Nope. "Breathless."

A crush on Richard Gere, I see.

I'm afraid so.

Someone she had often seen at the office, but had never spoken to, was seated on the bed perpendicular to them, playing a twelve-string guitar.

America, he had noted.

Yes. "A Horse with No Name."

And they had stood there, listening and not talking.

Two hours passing, fast and slow, and fatigue snuck in behind her eyes; they had become dry, and a migraine was on its way.

I have to go, she had told him, placing a quick kiss on each of his cheeks. Beer still in hand, he had looked at her, staring the way they all did. Eyes reddened by excess, eyes that said: I don't want to sleep. Or maybe I do. With you. She hadn't heard him ask her to stay, that the fun had just begun. To drink more. That he would take care of her.

No.

Walking toward Charlotte, wanting to tell her she was leaving, she had felt a hand wrap around her waist, pulling her back. It was nice to spend the summer with you in my vision, Adeline. Girls like you make it bearable for boys like me, you know, to stay.

Another one, she had thought, rolling her eyes.

Wiggling out of the forced embrace, and with the side of her hand mimicking the cutting of a throat, she had signaled to Charlotte she was done and leaving—now. Discreetly, feeling relieved, she had left and had walked the corridor leading to the outside staircase. Dawdling toward her trailer, she had looked up. The sun had started its descent an hour before, leaving sketches made of oranges and pinks on the northern firmament. The party had started early, she remembered thinking. A good thing.

It was the scent of alcohol that woke her, she realized from her seat. Keeping her eyes closed, she had thought it a dream until a weight pressed on the edge of her mattress.

Adeline, she had heard.

Above her, two faces.

She had lifted herself to a seated position, hugged her nightgown with one hand while pushing a man's torso away from her with the other, and she had laughed.

Stop it.

But girl, your door *was* unlocked.

Her eyes widened. The security guard responsible for the surveillance of her trailer, a woman, had left for the weekend.

A blanketed sensation. A soft violence, non-consensual.

The night, compressed, a failed fugitive, and at dusk, curled-up in her bed, wet and slimy, she had questioned the goal at the heart of heredity's purpose. It is flawed, she had concluded, it randomly pursues, ill aware, all things made of life and death. It will fool the world and its goodness, for there are no signs, physical signs, warning you that menaces are slinking. Blind spots—their den. She had tried to smile at her thought—it seemed so silly, if only they had been like the Kennedys. Because one sees them coming, their teeth giving them away—unavoidable icebergs—all of them, and for the next thousand years, it will be so. Yet, she had realized, I wasn't able to distinguish white souls from dark ones.

Holding her belly, her heart racing, she hears Bowie's tape cassette coming to an end, and she hears the whiteness of noise—its rhythm now gone, and then a quick transition to a voice telling her to come back and look. Through the porthole she notices the plane's right-side propeller gradually fall still. Four idle blades facing the wind, their stance remaining upright, and she soaks it in. No, she thinks. No.

She hears the men, their backs to her: a flash storm formed above the airport, Adeline. We need to circle the air further away from here, and we need to manage what is left of the fuel. So ... had to cut one engine out. But don't worry. We do that all the time. She says nothing, afraid of the past telling more than what reality is saying, now.

Whatever happened the night before she can't address—there's space inside of her head, too much space. She looks out again, sees water coming fast and steady, water and more water, too much of its detail, crisp and clear and so vivid.

Swirls, currents. Cold.

Guys, she wants to say, feeling paralyzed, look at me now. Reassure me like you do each week when you shuttle me from the main camp and back.

Both men are silent.

A soft panic settling in like an unavoidable presentiment.

The plane descending, and there's no land approaching.

She braces herself, grabs the arm of her chair, not understanding why when flying so low, nothing impacts them.

Adeline, hang on, we're landing.

There is no time to understand more of the moment life is bringing to her; she feels the plane hit the ground, hears it rumble to a complete stop.

The men cut the remaining engine and silence befalls the cockpit.

They remove their headsets and turn to her and say, all is good, that they've landed the Twin on an emergency landing strip built in the middle of the river. The Galina strip. They unbuckle their seatbelts, and she does the same, dazed.

Adeline has become pale—paler, her skin against the auburn of her locks. Let's step out and get some air, Adeline.

They lead the way, disembark, her behind.

Cold and nauseated, Adeline steps away from the plane and looks at the makeshift airfield. Everything in this land is makeshift, she whispers to herself. Even me. Too much is clashing inside of her. Is this what cheating death feels like? Two deaths, and still, I am breathing.

Adeline, they say, come over here.

They watch her walk toward them, benumbed, her hands shaking as she brings her hoody closer to her neck.

There is a boulder in her vision, and she focuses on it, using it as a compass. She walks to it. Leaning against the boulder, she says she's never asked his name. The oddness of it, she thinks, after all this time. Claude. And you? turning to the co-pilot. Daniel. How old are you, Claude? Twenty-eight. A bush pilot at twenty-eight, she whispers to herself. Me, Daniel adds, I'll be twenty-four next month—September 1.

Hum.

Yes, and I'm old enough to tell you that as much as you think this place is nothing, just look.

The river, wild and strong, surrounds them. The strip of land, like an amputated isthmus forming the only ground they can exist on, ground that doesn't ground her.

Will you be, okay?

I don't know, she says looking at both men.

Listen, Adeline, Claude says.

Her throat tightens and inside her body, certainty is trying to tunnel a way.

He takes her hand. The quiet is full, no?

The sobbing, uncontrollable, is soft, and while she feels the warmth of her tears wet her cheeks, she knows something else is at play. Yes, it is, she mumbles.

He takes her by the shoulders, tells her all will be okay, that microbursts, like anything that flashes, die quickly. Like an improvised pause.

As one who lives above, Daniel adds, pointing to the skies, it's about dealing with unpredictability, Adeline. That's all it is. Same goes for the ground, same rules.

She looks up at the sky, its never-ending repetitions of gray that rarely go away. Sometimes, she says, everything seems as one. Like there's no line on the horizon that I can really see. Like all is melting onto itself: one color, one smell, one image, one emotion, one sound.

And what do they feel all together?

I don't know. It fluctuates. Either I fuse with it, or I spit it back.

Well, I'll tell you this much, you can fuse with it, you can spit it out. Just don't ignore it.

She slowly pivots—a slow dance, a hand on the boulder and almost amused says they should be called the sky thinkers, that she can see a little better now. Everywhere she looks, these horizons encircling her, and they tell her to listen hard, to listen well, to know when to know—that this moment, crafted by circumstances that befriend only the strong, will not ever emerge again, that this moment is there to rest here, to go nowhere but now, in a tomb that lies against the current of a river soon to be diverted.

Listen and see.

The gushing of waves.

The soft tickling of the rain.

A sun ray escaping the clouds.

And did you know that your name is not Adeline? Claude asks, complicity in his eyes.

Her smile says she wants to understand. It is tentative. Hopeful.

And he tells the story of the declinations of a tone; of a color. This place.

Yes, he says as she holds on to his words—Duchess of Galina.

River Pools

This man moves slowly away from the door.

The night cold is with him; inside him.

It's still snowing out there, he tells her, and the river is still moving, as if it were summer.

From the kitchen sink, she looks out, pulls the curtain to the side and observes the river through the trees, the many ways it will never stop. She bends her head, absentmindedly washing the dishes, and whispers, that yes, the cold is still there, for now.

He keeps his coat on, wanting to warm his hands, wanting to slide them inside his pockets, but he can't—misses. I need to do this, he thinks, on my own. He tries again, closes his eyes, summons some form of breathing. Make me strong, he thinks, like I used to be. With a gait, stiff and weakening, he walks to her, wrists twisted, curled-up fingers stuck to his chest against his will. The hidden shakes.

A flash of beige-blonde hair, she stands. Her eyes want to give in, wet, but she won't let them. He needs strength, wherever it can come from. And please, God, don't let him see through me—the desperation inside my thoughts.

Dim the lights, won't you? And put some music on. White Rabbit.

She finds the song, presses play, and the music reaches him, ethereal—dazing, and he starts to unfold.

Half-drunk with sorrow, the other half winking at her as if it knew, maybe, life could become safe, and promising, like it was, and she dances, too, to a different rhythm.

Where is he at, she wonders, with that bent tallness in him.

When she touches him, stability returns, more, and it makes him want, the satin, the silk, the cashmere—love, unlaced, in the middle of a nowhere meant for the gone. Come my love, it's time to sleep.

The smell of morning floats to him, sinuous, strong. Unavoidable.

The challenge inside the start of the day where nothing that is him wants to obey; to live, even. He straightens his torso and swivels his feet to the ground, raises himself, imagines the ceiling reachable.

He walks to her, and she is waiting for him, as always.

A tray of multicolored pills on a small table set for two.

A fresh loaf of bread.

A stack of sliced pineapples.

A French-press.

Why did you come back, to this place?

Her face is shining. Alexander, my love, it's what I understand. And I followed you, didn't I? To this place I already knew...

Yes, he says, and I am grateful that you did. He looks to her, tired. Teach me, his eyes say, all that you know, how to be as of now—now that I will never be the same. Because the me that I know, I cannot seize anymore, it is slipping away from me. Help me, Charlotte.

More butter on your toast, she simply replies, taking his hand. It can bind, you know. She sips from the brittle cup, drippings of madness in her coffee, and she thinks, yes, another peaceful breakfast with crumbs of uncertainty carpeting existence.

It had started the year before, she recalls, unheeded warnings, legs giving out, rickety and unforgiving, arms threatening to swing oddly, rigor inside knowing hands.

Then, the slur, erasing all traces of past eloquence, a mouth that wouldn't follow the brain.

It didn't make sense, none of it did.

Impossible. Too young. So, so young. Forty-four.

Has to be anxiety. Fatigue most certainly. A wicked flu.

Not *that*—Parkinson, *my* man.

Spring slowly came, to vanish but quickly, turning into a volatile summer made of winter—carrying with it, a warmer sun; a warmer river.

Inside this place—the north of all norths, the taiga of all taigas.

The morning still, more demanding, never giving. The never-failing reminder.

He opens the door, and lets the cool air in, wanting none of it.

Baby come, she says. The smoker needs to be washed, it smells of soot more than anything else, and of burnt fish, too. The Suburban, also, needs cleaning. We can't even make out the blue of its doors.

The last fishing trip comes to his mind, more than a year before. The smell of beer and fuel. The laughter inside the belly of men, content and mindful, the zodiac filled with nervy salmon wanting to reach back to the waters, looking for rapids to jump over. Like me, he thinks, my own rapids.

I must show her.

He takes one step onto the patio, and he loses his balance. He falls another fall, and this time she witnesses, sees—weaknesses, alive and well, and squeezing juices from his mouth.

But the next day is made of a sun he sees and feels again, and he shows her he still can.

Walk. Talk. Play.

Baby, just hose the top, yeah, like that.

She lets him, lets him pretend he is capable of normality. Equilibrium.

They laugh like forgetful escapees, drops of water falling on them, almost freezing.

He takes her hand. Hers trembling, too. Because frailty is contagious even to those who don't dare to look.

Standing, crooked and contorted, in the middle of a gravel-made driveway, he tries to hide.

She looks on. Straight on.

The unfairness, so quiet, at the centre of their life. And Adeline's face materializes before her, a red-headed ghost that should have never been one. You know cold, harshness, Adeline, and I wish you were with me so you could feel the harshness of this one. It will never melt. She looks to him. Come, she says, let's go back inside. Our bedroom.

Heads lopsided, manes entangled, they laugh, in the middle of the bed.

We are, aren't we?

Reaching for her face, eager and shaky, he spills the wine glass on her white dress.

It's okay, she always says. I'll go change and slip a red one on this time.

When she comes back to him, he is crying, his hands having become fists wringing out most of what is left of his strength.

Let me help. She quietly straightens each of his fingers then kisses his forehead with a mouth eager to soothe. Yes, here, she says as she pops the buttons out of their holes, removes the shirt, throwing it to the floor.

The monogram, she sees. Faded, unthreaded. Him.

Rest.

Under the sheets, he thinks of these traps that press for unwanted answers to the surface. They mind-fuck. All falls do. He thinks of his career; of the stellar status he holds inside the vast world of engineering; of the millions that swim inside his bank accounts; of God; of the sickness of believing in Him—for why would He have planted this seed of decay inside of him? I will get even. I have no choice. I will dictate. I will let Him know the ending will not be under His control. My legacy will be to trip Him; to trip his mistress, Fate.

The pub is dark and empty but for them. J.J. Cale's voice is coming out of the speakers. The place feels like a cold velour—like what it is.

You will do as I want, he softly tells them, pushing his beer aside.

These friends, tempted to flee his contortions, listen.

He smiles. I want you to tell me when you think I will die, predict my death.

A pool, one of them whispers.

Exactly.

They smile, shake their heads, and agree to play, each one writing different dates meant to foretell his ending.

The tallest one, drunk but aware, places the stack of napkins in Alexander's shaky hands.

Inside the small parlor, he walks in the next day.

Here, he says to the tattoo artist, all those years, in order.

January 21 2025

April 2 2026

June 17 2028

February 2 2029

April 17 2029

December 25 2030

Black ink on muscle-stretched biceps: a fuck you to the world.

A dead pool meant for the living. Plain and simple.

And soon, one million dollars to the lucky one beating God at the business of death.

From their balcony she points down, to the valley. The waters' movements are slow, she tells him. Don't you think there's a welcoming anaemia, a rare one, inside of its motion today?

Seated beside her on the porch overlooking the river, he says that he wants it, that water is a place for him to hide in, the place to trick himself and the whole world. That's what you are to me, Charlotte: water. So much of your liquid love running inside my veins.

Yes, I know, Alexander. Let me pull you in that stream, believe, she thinks.

And for a moment, the briefest of them, he does, plowing through his desire to fight it.

All of it.

But they leave, don't they? Certainties, however soft and seductive. He points to the sky as he presses against her small body. No one wants to add to my body. No one wants to risk more of my skin with their thoughts; their own certainties.

Can you blame them? And you have enough of those dates anyway.

Yes, I can. Because there is just one possible outcome, isn't there? A young death. And so much to win. They lack conviction, Charlotte. The conviction that lies at the heart of my game. It is not their death, it is mine, no? And they owe me—everything their life is made of: hooks; strolls; fucks. I want to kill them for what I have lost, what I am losing. With guilt. And since I can't, they should play with me. One last time.

She kisses his cheek, and turns to him, observing his face. So inexpressive, as if paralyzed, she thinks, the sickness has taken hold of his face.

Will I burn the same, he wonders out loud. Will I burst into more fire because of this shaky defiance?

You are retreating like an old and sick wolf, Alexander, she says as she scoops him up gently, the tremors and the non-tremors.

Follow me. You said you wanted water …

He lets her, and slides into the bathtub.

The water is hot. Not enough, he thinks.

Her eyes cling to him.

I love you, he manages to say, words that not so long ago glided from the mouth of a bard now filled with a rhythm that only stutters into her heart. It's okay. I can do it.

I know, Alexander, we know how to move with it.

Winters that stretch and barely leave, succeed themselves. The spruce remain, tall and straight and crooked, almost balding, their needles long and thin, their spread, sparse.

One by one the prophecies come and go, discarded by time. Dates meant to predict his passing, now erased, and demanding more from the future.

And the river, too, still flows, uninterrupted by its own essence.

She looks to it.

Then, a day like so many others, not too far from then, when, by the sink, she will pull the curtains apart, and stare at the river again.

Small tides imitating the sea. Trying to.

It means nothing, she will know, absolutely nothing.

And inside her, shivers and slivers of wishes heaving.

She will refill, watching the red flow as she tilts the glass a little more, watching it coat the transparency of a dulled-out shine.

Her finger caressing its rim.

There will be movement behind her, and it won't startle her. She will grab his hands, bringing them to her chest. Look, she will say, pointing to the stack of money always ready and waiting at the end of the kitchen counter.

Still here.

Like you.

She will slowly flip through it, as if it were a deck of tricked cards, then bring the glass to his lips.

Taste, she will murmur. It's your favorite year.

Bloomers Contemplating (more) Starvation

THE HOUSEMASTER HAS GONE to bed, satisfied—all the girls are back in their rooms.

Inside the second story of the school dormitory, music reaches her from the neighboring room, some giggles and soft crying, too. A usual silence is whispered, black-noised, and she knows they all miss home. They must.

I do.

Wiggling naked inside the thin plastic sheet she has tightly wrapped herself into, and lying on her back, she turns her head to look at the girl sleeping across her bed. Heather. The tall and slender blonde is breathing slowly, and the scent of her is lingering inside their room; it will until the end of the school year—Yves Saint-Laurent's nauseating Opium.

Adeline gets up from her bed, clenching the pliable material around her waist, and carefully moves toward the large window located one foot from her bed. Pushing the curtain to one side, she looks on to the soccer field spread before her, the school buildings her life will be tied to for a second year, too. A last year. Leaves are twirling, and trees are shedding past colors from their boughs and their twigs. When she looks at the autumn spectacle, she is unmoved—images of snow appear, thoughts of home spin inside her mind. Michi. Her father.

Mom.

Thanksgiving weekend is behind her, and she thinks of the Christmas holidays, and of the eight weeks standing between now and her Inukshuks.

Heather stirs and words come out of her mouth. Looking down to where she sleeps, Adeline listens, trying to decode the story her roommate only shares with the night, unaware of the antennae capturing fragments of her narrative. We all have them, Heather, she thinks. Narratives. And yours is so common around here. Insipid, really. You, the daughter of the American ambassador to Arabia, the daughter your parents conveniently dropped inside a world made of your kind—for your kind. A gnarly peer group—children who will grow from the certainties rank and money provide. You are obsessed with your acne (who wouldn't be?), convinced your Clinique products will chase the burgeons off your narrow and oily face. You feel a hard crush for the headmaster's son who will play you until tired of your smell and your preppy look, your princess-like airs. You are just one of many. Vulgar tinder.

I'm hungry, Adeline thinks as she slides back into bed, her fingers following the dampness contouring her bony body. Her hands find the concave of her stomach and when they do, she smiles. I'm hungry, she thinks. But I ate yesterday. My binging day. She turns her attention to Heather again, feeling triumphant over the genesis of a disappearance, this life-giving plastic that makes her sweat, inducing calorie burning meant to please a young girl eager to control her life—her narrative. Not enough kids her age wandering in her caribou-filled land, she repeats in her mind. I was sent here because seventh grade is where it stopped for me. She recalls, her school, the small building, a hovel made of adjoining trailers that smelt of old J-Prock and overheated air that tried to battle the cold. A lost wintery war. I was sent here, me, a French Canadian who barely can speak English. I am here breathing the same stale air as my establishment-born Anglo princess. But you should know, I, too, am celebrity by association, she lets out. I am the daughter of John Brodeur, the manipulator of water. The creator of currents.

I can hear you, you know, she hears Heather say.

Go back to sleep, Heather. It's 11:45. And so you know, I'm glad you can hear me.

Still, tears roll into her mouth, and she turns her body toward the wall. Pinned to it and looking at her is the school calendar, the October page flipped open, each past day marked with an 'X'. Tomorrow is Sunday, she sees. And the tears dry, and the smile reappears. Go to sleep, Adeline Brodeur.

When she awakens, Heather is still sleeping, and a filmy white light comes through the window, and the movement of falling leaves shadow dance on the industrial carpeting. She stares at their play for a while, then slowly unfolds to the coming day. Standing, she turns and confronts the bed— kneels before it, as if it were an altar. Her arm stretched under the bed, her cheek hugging the floor, her fingers recognize the cold metal of the scale. Pulling it out, she stands and places it before the bedroom door onto which a full-length mirror hangs. Her eyes are closed, and she slides her feet one at a time on her truth-teller. One minute passes and she exhales, head bent, eyes to her new number. Replacing the scale underneath her bed, a feeling of vitality embraces her. The lighter the body, the lighter the mind. Time for a shower.

Opening her small closet, she removes the components of her Sunday attire from the hangers. Her throat is knotted, and she dresses slowly, the absentee in her emerging, and looking at the soccer field still empty and green-grassed.

An ill-fitted gray skirt, baggy and dangling below her hipbones, a white, puffy blouse, a blue blazer inside which she loves to swim—hide. In the mirror, her permed hair falls to her shoulders, still dripping from her showering. In her eyes, for all to ignore, the comforts of intimate and physical losses root farther, deeper. Her pounds. She nods with approval of this thinness matching the hate for her life here, a campus conceived for the intentionally abandoned. She walks the corridor of her dormitory, and the path to the main school building. She enters the dining hall, a cold Victorian wood-made embrace. An orange food tray in hand while carrying a tall glass of cold water, and a crisp Macintosh apple rolls across the tray, threatening to drop. The shakings of her body reemerge, her mind's, too.

Breakfast is eaten alone and when it is done, she stands and walks to where the trays are returned, sliding hers away. As she leaves, she watches the students line up outside the hall; they are ready to climb the stairs leading up to the chapel. Sunday Mass and her weekly escapes are ready for their debut.

She walks past the line of students, a large, floppy bag across her back, the one she recouped from inside the yellow clusters located adjacent to the dining hall. They look at her, the curiosity her body has become, the kinks of her hair, and when she hears one boy calling her a walking mop, she ignores him, their stares, too.

Outside the clouds hang low, and the day's unusual heat won't reach her flesh. A cold skinniness, and she huddles inside her blazer—she will huddle inside of it until she reaches her destination.

The others, French Canadians like her, are waiting for her on the steps of the entrance building. Boys and girls, her own age, dressed in pale grays and dark blues and wearing their Sunday school ties. You got your dispensation, too, she hears. They all laugh at their scheme and its success. This genius idea. So easy, she says, shy-smiled, and eyes to the ground.

I did what you told me to do.

Suddenly feeling alert, she tells them her story, innocuous yet charged with victory's arrogance, of how the old, white-collared man made of Protestant hiccups looked at her with eyes slit and serious, framed by white and unruly brows, of how she told him proudly she was a good little French Canadian Catholic school girl, and that she wouldn't mind to continue attending the daily fifteen-minute morning school Mass, but that on Sundays, Reverend, 'I will attend to my faith. I miss the Holy Communion, you see.' Yes. The Sunday morning hunger, novel and deceptive, for freedoms that live inside a blessed wafer she won't bother to stick up to her palate. Eat.

The group of students leave the main school building and walk down the road leading them off the campus. The football field to their right is empty. So, too, are the tennis courts to their left. Later, she thinks.

The town bridge linking their world to a normalcy they crave appears, and they walk to it, and when her foot first touches the deck, she slides the bag off her back. Go on without me, she says, I'll meet you inside. Her hesitant fingers searching inside the bag, her hand retrieves a pack of cigarettes and an open bottle of Irish whiskey. She lights up, takes a swig, and returns the items to the bag. The half-smoked cigarette hangs between her still-trembling fingers, and she walks on. It's been ten minutes since she's left the school grounds, and she understands, the farther away she exists from its manicured façade, the better she can sense—her core dropping like congealed lava sinking into bedrock, an earth she can now recognize.

The shakings fade.

She waits beside the church located on the edge of the small town, and looking on, she observes a dozen parishioners standing on the church square. Sunday dresses, coiffed heads, kid-gloved hands—the women smell of impeccability, of righteousness, too. The few men she sees are huddled together, smoking and impatient for the service to start—finish—so they can return to their homes, she thinks, and continue with the day's inbred pace, slow and still. The priest dressed in true black wrings his hands, an affable smile, honest and welcoming, sitting on his face, and from the short distance existing between beliefs and dues, she hears from the wind, of its carrying—tones and sounds made of her. The French language. Her college friends, are about to enter, and she waves to them. Meet me at the end of the service, she lips-synchs, and pointing to the marquee of the pizzeria located across the church. They nod with eyes that understand, and when they do, Adeline is elsewhere, ready for an exit—for a gate.

The doors are too heavy for her weak frame and she doesn't have the strength to push them open. She lets her body fall backward, as if a dancer trusting her partner will catch her, just in time, teasing gravity, that he is reliable, that he won't drop her to the floor. Hurt her. She wins the battle, and when she enters the restaurant, the fragrance of unfood comes for her, umami scents her brain quickly responds to. Her tongue tingling, her stomach whetted, she feels it talk. It knows to find me, but she punches it—a mental punch. Shrink, she tells it.

She continues to the far end of the dining room and chooses to sit at a table located next to the window overlooking the church. The waitress comes and she orders a black coffee—the blood of my god, she tells her, with a smile. A long second travels inside the waitress' eyes, and she tells her, yes, that for her, too, it's the best blood ever.

Adeline remains seated, pushing twirls of smoke from her mouth and staring beyond her so-called Lord's home. Parcels of calm want to settle into her, to sway inside her young mind. Yet as she sips her coffee, the lack of belonging she experiences, soft and loose, morphs into a tight and leash-like sensation. She closes her eyes, shakes her head and wonders, how much longer will I be able to survive this place? Am I even able to?

Time moving fast, and she knows to look at her watch, the hour sprained by the wringing of her northern guises. Visions of cold-filled remembrances: lichened soils, white waters, and skies dancing with light—so much grace. The sound of someone knocking on the window startles her, prompting her to lift her head. Yes, she mouths to the school girl. I need to settle the bill. Two minutes.

As she walks twenty feet past the church, her friends dawdling ahead of her, she stops in front of the local watering hole. The Lion's Pub. The balcony is filled with patrons eating their lunches. Music is sounding. Supertramp. Neil Young. Bob Dylan. She hears her friends calling out for her to hurry up, that lunch is being served at school, that if they miss the sign-in, they'll have to run laps, or worse, get the strap. They can't see, but she is smiling. Go on, she yells again. I'll be fine. *I'll be fine.*

The door is ajar—inviting, and when she walks into the bar, the smell of rancid beer greets her, and she feels hunger tugging at her a little more than before. Scanning the empty room, she hops onto one of the five barstools bolted along one side of the horseshoe-shaped bar. The nineteen-year-old bartender observes her from behind the wood counter, and when he does, the girl's eyes widen, and she thinks, do I know you? The young man, tall and wide, turns to the glass shelves floating above his head, chooses a cheap bottle of vodka, and a hurricane glass. You look older than you are, and I know I shouldn't serve you, he says as he prepares the drink, but just this once, okay? A Bloody Caesar. Seems you could use some. And it's Sunday after all. Time for brunch.

He slides the glass in front of her, and she stares at it, a debate tumbling in her head. The celery stick. The spiced-up rim. The blood-orange, viscous concoction.

You don't know it, but I'm from the future, little girl, he laughs. The young man extends an arm, gently takes her hand, and brings it to his lips. The kiss is just as gentle, and when he places it back on the bar, she can see something has settled inside of him. A tranquility. You've been there, and I have, too, he continues. That's how you recognize me. You do, don't you? I can see it in your eyes.

His face reminds me of a Dorian Gray I've seen and imagined in the past. A variation of his beauty. She rubs her hand, feels the wetness he left behind. Sees it stamped atop it.

A long silence follows, the lightness of time to come inside future-bound seconds, and him staring at her—him.

You're a student … What is it you study?

History. Political science. Double major.

Her eyes become glued to his.

I do know, he goes on with a smile, one day, Frenchie, you'll come back to this place, with me, and order a couple of those Caesars, and we'll leave, and feeling tipsy you'll walk the streets of this town again, a mix of nostalgia and non-understandings sinking in your heart, and you'll start to wiggle as you laugh, your bladder brimming with liquids and you'll say, wait C.P., I gotta go now, and you'll run to the back of that pizza joint, outside, and you'll relieve yourself in the skinny bushes bordering the parking lot.

She smiles. Wow. You can see all of that?

Yes, I can. Gypsy blood, it's called.

Okay, then. What's my name?

I don't know, Adeline Brodeur, what is it?

Her mouth opens a smile, and she looks at him, taken. Gypsy blood. Funny, she says, I've always wanted to be one. A gypsy.

You're one already. You've just never acknowledged it.

Yeah. Maybe it's true. And when is all this is supposed to occur …?

Forty-three years from now.

Hum. Forty-three years is a long time, no?

Worth the wait. You'll see. I know. And please, don't ever lose the French accent. You can grow to be the woman I know you will become. But promise you will never change that.

A long silence stretches, and she plays with her drink, removing the celery stick from the liquid, leaving the glass full. She looks at her watch. It's been over an hour, she says, surprised. I need to go back. I guess I'll be seeing you …

When the right times come, baby girl.

She jumps from the stool, places her bag across her body, and walks to the door. Merci, she says, turning back around, whoever you say you are, *C.P.*, and yet there is no one there, no tall and wide man standing, only the celery-less Caesar she left untouched. As she scans the room more, frissons run up and down her limbs, reminding her cold is being fabricated by her body, that she is feeding upon herself. Starvation-fed hallucinations, she concludes. Has to be.

The walk back to the world is slow, dreamful. Reaching the bridge, her curls move in the wind, her eyes squinting into the pale sun, and she feels lightness she forgot existed.

The stick of celery between her teeth, she climbs back up the road leading to the main building. The football field is filled with boys running plays, the tennis courts with girls practicing their serves. And again, she thinks, maybe later.

She ignores the main building, walking directly back to her boarding house.

She climbs the short set of stairs to the second floor, foot-dragging to her room. When she opens the door, the princess is seated in a lotus position, a book spread across her knees, a greenish cosmetic mask covering her face. You missed lunch.

I'm good, she says, pointing to the celery stick.

They were looking for you, you know. Five laps in the morning, the housemaster said. He knows you can't do more. The whole school knows, you know ...

Remaining silent, Adeline Brodeur removes her clothing, the image of the young man imprinted in her young mind. His eyes, they carried beliefs, she thinks, and she is certain she has seen them before, and that face, somewhere—but where? The future, he said. Smiling, she whispers to herself, should be promising. She looks at her hand, sees the slight mark left by the liquid's evaporation.

She chooses a pink sweatshirt to wear on which The Kinks is written in large, plump letters, and she drops onto her bed. Famishment is pinching her body, and she thinks of her next meal, the binging party for one—next Friday night. I love running, Heather, Adeline suddenly says. I live for runs. Their power to flesh out. She turns to the wall, picks a pen from the desk behind her, and crosses the day's date from the calendar, and she circles the Friday next to come. What I dislike, though, she continues as she turns toward the green-faced girl, is the smell of your perfume, Heather. I hate the smell of other people's opium. She pauses, looking into the girl's eyes, ignoring the discomfort, then turns to the ceiling, her head sinking into the pillow. Her thoughts are hard, unpliable. My opium is made of frost, and the weaning from that is killing me. I know. Her eyelids drop, and she summons his razor-sharp cheeks to appear—ritualistic incantations now born: the mane of black hair, hazel eyes, and she will forever wait for them, and their kindness. But I can't let the weaning win—kill me. I need to survive forty-three years more, whether in the warmth or the cold of my life. So I can see you again, my gypsy boy.

And I did.

Bleeding Dyad

The pain, this feeling of inadequacy, is there with you, and although the seed of it was never recognized as a seed belonging to it, as a seed made of it—pain, they planted it still, in your making, ignorance at the centre of their manufactured bliss, this justification—they didn't know; did their best.

But you, you do, now. Know. Should understand. Still, you remain tongue-tied as much as heart-chained. Is it a brain thing? A personality disordered—forever?

All I wanted was for you to be my witness, and me, yours. The ultimate witness, Coco, one that would be forever present; a memory, different, yet validating, this gift, accessible until death.

No.

You arrived five years after I was born. You arrived with eyes already slanted; with eyes that would rival the green of mine, with skin already hinting of a pigmentation unknown to our genes, like some exotic human all leaned over with acceptable lust.

The pictures of you speak to me.

You arrived on a day befitting as much as telling—Halloween night. An early winter storm pushing autumn leaves into the air, tearing ripe stems from their branches, and Mom was in the hospital preparing for you to arrive. But I don't remember—any of it. I don't remember Mom being pregnant, the blooming of you in a body toxified by nicotine, foul thinking; some form of mental illness. I don't remember Dad fussing over the impending arrival of trouble, this soon to be you: intelligent and beautiful trouble.

The pre-prandial leading to you was never heeded.

I was with our grandparents, at their home, babysat by our aunt, my godmother. I didn't know I was waiting for you. No words resound in the box that hold my memories. But memory is like a bohemian, isn't it? It plays the music it wants to hear; it dances with trickery—it steals, too. I suppose there was an energy that night, a prolepsis, with the promise of new scents and feels, the soon to be discovered features of a newborn, newly etched features to muse over. Such hope is placed upon each of our entrances.

You were not spared that hope.

My only concern that night was to become gypsy-like, to trot the narrow streets of a small French Canadian village with a leopard-printed turban on my head and blue-laden eyelids and pink lipstick painting my five-year-old face. This obsession, my only want: to slide into a costume that would make me feel noticed; make me more. I often wonder, when revisiting this eve of your coming, how it was the virus had successfully been injected into my nascent mind. This disease, the feeling of not being enough, a seed like an ovule.

I guess we each caught one.

It was cold that night, the winds, turbulent, and the few lampposts planted along some of the streets—I see them still, swaying, and snow, like white-winged moths fluttering to the light. Such vividness. A rare one. Our aunt insisted I slide my dress over a snowsuit, a blue puffed up winter attire, ill-formed and grotesque to my precocious sense of aesthetics. I threw myself on the linoleum of the kitchen floor in a rage, legs and arms batting, I was told. Held my breath. Became blue. I was sent to bed. My remembrance of you, the prologue of you, never existed. Unlike you, this little you I got to meet two days later, Mom walking inside Grandmother's kitchen, Dad in tow. Surprised, I didn't understand, this stranger, there—what? now, noisy—idle. And Mom's smile, a Mona Lisa-esque grin sketched across the bottom of her face with eyes that seemed dead. Dad walking up to me, a yellow and purple Fischer-Price fishing rod in his hand. Here, Adeline, she brought you a gift.

She?

I've searched Coco, so often, and still do—the answers always coming, hypotheses, reevaluated always, the disbelief equal to the grief—about this lack of foundation between us, and I wonder, if you do, too, understand why we were never capable of playing; of caring; of laughing; of loving, as sisters.

After your birth—six months later, came our move to Churchill Falls, Labrador, a then satellite town that would become a permanent fixture in a landscape of rectangular trailers, metal-sided and white, standing on soils, and the hard, granular sands I played in, always dressed in some Sears catalog-wear Mom ordered from the comfort of her small kitchen, cigarette hanging from her large mouth. And from that trailer we should have called home, a bond never formed, for you and I were baptized by the cold, Coco, by the subarctic's constant simmers, the relentlessness of the boreal climate.

The sun, anyhow—always so deceptive.

A photograph of us, I come back to it, often. Our living room, pre-furnished like the rest of the trailer, a couch made of dark colonial wood, upholstered with green and orange polyester fabric that reeked of smoke. Kneeling on the cushions, you in my arms, we are facing one another: two sisters wearing the same onesies, white and red Christmas pajamas, me holding you, your eyes melting into mine as I tie the thin ribbon underneath your chin.

What happened, Coco?

No memory of you anywhere we lived. A blank the color of dry, icy snow, banks of it, taller than you and me.

The permafrost won and has followed us everywhere once your existence came to be recognized—remembered now, by me, a witness' account.

The gaze I see in that photograph, so trusting—it disappeared, it seems. I don't know when it died, as I don't recall.

Remember?

The smell of your baby hair, the kisses, the holding—a non-start; my senses, numb.

The truth had to be sculpted out, time its knife—what I know now follows me like diced-up shivers we came to life from. For years now, this forever malice sparkling in your green eyes, a light that whispers of somber—the world around me seeing it: family, strangers, telling me about the predator in you, this capacity to betray love, closeness, intimacy. And your smile, epicaricacy living on a face blessed with symmetry around which hair, black and straight, frames your paragon. Christie Turlington, they said, each time my friends met you. A beautiful Algonquian-like woman, too. And me, fair-skinned, freckled-faced, and frizzled, rustled hair like a large, brimmed hat waving around my head, rusty looking. Yet, I never envied you. Same green eyes, though. But yours were always greener, Coco. Your heart like a snake, mine like a lost leprechaun's.

As absurd as it sounds, when one looks for answers, anywhere, and nowhere, delineating hope as a mirage capable of quelling—I have wondered, wanting to be wrong, is narcissism the burglar?

My own features—were they the source of a hatred meant to stay? I've wondered for some time now, had they spoken to you—too loud, and saying what? Do you remember? Me walking to the dog's crate and picking up one of her puppies, the narrow space adjacent to Dad's stereo, the shelves made of thin, tempered glass. Your foot, you dragged so very slowly, the lazy motion of a child's nonchalant being, yet all too studied in front of me—you tripped me. It was quick, painless, my fall, headfirst into the shelves, the broken shelves, shards of glass planted into the fabric of the thick carpeting. The noise alerted her, and Mom appeared from the hallway, at first angry at being interrupted—she was playing solitary, I think—but then a grimace distorted her mouth. I thought it was because I had been the cause of the mess. No. My face. My left cheek, diagonally sliced three-inch-long and one-inch deep. My forehead, too, a two-inch horizontal cut. The soft trickle of warm blood dripping on my face. Then, her yells. You will be disfigured for the rest of your life. On repeat. It didn't hurt then. Only when the scar tissue started to thicken did the pain settle inside the centre of my cheek. My forehead, too.

Years later, and the hope that all of it is imagination.

The ground we grew from, the only culprit.

It must be.

I speak to Dad about us, you know, regularly, a tragedy for him. Mom, as well. The sisters that could never be. The family broken even before they broke it for real. He blames it on her, you know. The storm was always her, he said—words brewed from inside a man-fed mind and sharpened by religious dogmas—never the indulgences, the many reoccurring ones, philandering realities rationalized and stoking her fragile mind.

I was conceived with love, that I know, coming into the world a wanted human; wanted for my innocence; wanted, for they had something to give.

Do you know why you were conceived, Coco?

Two years ago, seated across from one another, a bottle of Argentinian red splitting the table, Dad told me, the marriage was wobbly and fight-filled, and I do remember before you became cogitation, flying dishes, screams, tears, physical fights, as a one-year-old, a two-year-old, three-year-old. Me, the witness. So many tears, and the yelling coming from her. Distraught, he sought advice from his father, this human of the land only. The answer coming from the farmer's mouth was quick: Make her another baby—a peasant's guide to survival.

Think of it, Coco, you owe your life to that moment.

A piece of the puzzle—surely, another insanity in the making.

This impossible mission drawn up and placed inside flawed thinking, inside our mother's belly. And when the thought was formed, filled with nothing more than a weight no one should ever carry, unfair, and cruel, Dad wanted to leave Mom for another woman whose husband had died; whose husband shared the same birthday as his; whose daughter carried the same name as mine, born on the same day, too. Deceitful serendipity. They set you up, born to fail, a failure having been laid upon you, from before you were soft flesh and malleable bone. And were you not ... seen just as a thing? Dead on arrival, your soul?

I am no better than you, Coco—I think of myself as a failure, and yet, what is my excuse?—born from love, I still was unable to keep them together.

And I lost you.

I still hope, Coco, that you will someday learn to untie your tongue; unchain your heart and set it free.

Do not let the cold win, more, Coco, and come and revisit us—and just us, and not them, somewhere, some-time, on warmer ground.

And my perch will be, this way of existing for me, now—words.

These words. Will you take them?

You've been sitting here silent for the better part of the session. We have fifteen minutes left before the end of the hour. Is there something you would like to leave me with?

A part of me does. The other part wants to go.

Ah. Your voice. It's calmer now. You seemed agitated earlier. You mentioned something about a letter. Would you like to talk about that?

I'm not sure I can just now.

All right then. Is this your first time?

I've seen some of your kind a couple of times in the past.

Our kind ...

Well, you know, the so-called helping kind.

Right. And thank you for giving me a chance to hear you out. The last time was ...?

I get tongue-tied, until I don't. The last I finished was two years ago.

It lasted ...?

Both times were CBT in spirit. Both of them, extra-small terms. Turns out it should have been long-termed interventions.

Because ...

I'm here. And you're a known figure in the guru world of help.

You're here because of curiosity.

I'm everywhere because of it.

Okay. For curiosity's sake, how would you like to leave today's session?

What do you mean?

How do you want to feel when you leave my office to-day?

I want to leave knowing you find me attractive.

I'll pretend I didn't hear that.

It was a joke.

You switch gears fast, I see ... Glad to hear it's a joke. Now...

It's a small order for today, Dr. Einstein.

It's Rubenstein.

Yeah. I know that, too.

I see where this is not going. Let me help y—

Light. I want to feel lighter.

Thank you, Coco. So, working with me will be about working with yourself. You're accountable for your progress. I put in the work if you put in the work as well. Team work.

Short-term?

Coaching is usually a short-term intervention, yes. A goal and process oriented one. Still, I'm a psychiatrist, too. And I'm a big fan of everything humanistic, the humanist school of thought. A big influence. I like to think that when you put them all together, it's a good combo. Let's say my process is in the middle of short and long.

No short-term, then.

Whatever term. I want my patients to be functional. They are functional when they no longer need me.

I understand.

Why did you consult in the past?

They all had to do with work. Work-related issues.

Okay. How would you qualify the sessions you had?

It doesn't stick. Once I reach the fourth session, I can't seem to go on. Pursue. I become mute. I qualify them as failures, I guess.

I see. What has changed since then?

I think I'm ready to find out ... what it is that's wrong with me.

You weren't before?

That's pretty much my understanding.

What triggered you wanting to seek help the last times?

Compliance, to be honest. Pressured by work. Employee-assistance programs. The proverbial gun to one's head.

And this time?

The same.

Are you sure?

Let's pretend I am for now.

All right. Let's get the basic down, shall we?

Fine by me.

Married?

Yes. Twelve years.

Kids?

Four. All girls. Twins, ten, Chloe and Josephine. Cara, seven. Marianne, five.

What do you do for a living?

I float from job to job. Keep getting fired. Behavior problems they all say.

They say ... You don't seem to agree.

Depends on the day. That said, I've been in agreement with that since the week before I called you for an appointment.

What were the issues?

Hum. Let me think ... Before an audit I knew was coming, I *mishandled* corporate documents—I work in HR. I forgot to have a few employees sign their onboarding document, had them sign a year later, told them not to tell anyone. Well, they told on me. Then, my last job, I came in drunk to the office one time too many. Lots of flirting, as well. Married men. High-profile married men. Oh, a fight, too. Someone's wife, at the workplace. A hard-core bitch slap.

Hum. Do you consider yourself to be a violent person?

Difficult to deny that I am with what I just shared. Yes, I can be, but not so often. With men usually. Hitting a woman was a first.

With words, too?

In that field, Dr., I'm the best.

On the onboarding thing, it seems a bit benign. Why didn't you just go and explain to your boss? We all make mistakes.

Because my performance review wasn't all that good already ... I was flagged. On probation.

It puzzles me. It's a simple post-dating thing. Easily understood.

The in-house lawyer didn't think so. My view on things, my genuine lack of transparency, she said. A question of integrity.

Where was this?

I can't say but imagine a big, big accounting firm.

This was your last job.

Yes.

Why did you get in a fight?

The woman showed up in my office. Couldn't stop yelling. She was out of control. I slapped her too hard, I guess. Lucky for me, she didn't press charges.

I would say. You had a thing with her husband.

The CEO.

Betrayal, that type of hurt can unleash a storm.

They weren't happily married anyway. I think I did them a favor.

Ah. And your husband knows, about your affairs?

No. I keep my side-pieces well hidden.

Even this time around?

So far, yes.

What does your husband do?

Colin is a civil engineer, works for the government. Hydro.

Do you think that you have a drinking problem?

A small one, I suppose. Wine.

You sound like you understand quite well what the trouble is.

I don't know the source, though. How to stop it, mostly.

You want to stop.

I'm here, aren't I? My girls ...

You want to do it for them—get better.

I suppose I do. I have always been in love with the number four, unlike the Asians I look like. I was always fascinated by families that had four children. The ones I know of seem stable, loving. Exempt from turmoil. The magic number. Always four.

But not for you.

No.

I see your eyes ... something different.

Don't worry, I rarely cry.

Hum ... okay .... What is your occupation now?

Not employed at the moment.

Right. And when you float from job to job, what job is it we're talking about?

I'm in HR, like I told you. Remunerations. Pensions Fund. Numbers are my game.

You like to play with them.

Very much.

And you work with people ...

A big problem. It seems I'm not so good with "people relations."

Why HR, then?

My undergrad, a double major. Mathematics and Economy. I needed to go on to a higher level of study for a chance to have a career in that. But didn't feel like keeping on in uni. I started in recruitment. I had friends who were making lots of money in recruitment. Head-hunting jobs. I started there, and tried to steer toward my forte, numbers.

Okay. Lots to work with here. Good work, that is.
Glad you think so.
You're not here just because of work issues, are you?
True.
All right, good. Are you up for homework?
Do I have a choice?

Of course, you do, and you know it. It may help you reach beyond the fourth session ...

I'm familiar with the concept of wasted time, Dr. Rubenstein. I'll give it a go. Besides, you're not cheap.

All right, then, Coco. This is what I would like you do, if possible: From a quiet place, anywhere—somewhere in your house, a coffee shop, a park—I want you to find a moment in your life—it doesn't have to be recent; it doesn't have to be from deep in your past either, it's what-ever speaks to you—when you felt in control of yourself. Where and when you have touched it. Control. A good feeling of control. Then, I want you to take this time be-tween now and our next session to think about what you really want to achieve here with me. Write one goal down that seems realistic, that you would like to reach.

How does one measure these types of goals, Dr.?

Interesting—no one ever asked that before. My yard stick is about what lives inside of you. What comes out.

Emotions.

Call it that ... is all okay?

I don't feel any lighter.

When she walks inside the house, water dripping from the brim of her hat, her coat soaked with rain, the girls are seated at the dinner table, a board-game spread across it, unaware of their mother's return. Coco watches them from the entrance—this order. The wine has rushed into the stream of her; she skips dinner. Hey girls, she says, I'll be in my room. Chloe, you're in charge.

She climbs the stairs, a hand gripping the ramp, and reaches the landing. From there, with tentative feet, she walks into a bedroom still alive with light, her eyes finding the unmade bed. Quickly, she undresses and drops her clothing onto the floor. The covers are twisted and bunched at the foot of the bed, and she pulls them to her neck. Right, she thinks as she flicks the bedside lamp off, and closes her eyes—the boardgames, and she remembers: She had short bangs hanging straight from her head high above her eyes, a page-like hairdo, and her right eye had started to wander. Still wearing her snow-pants, she sat in the family room and from underneath the bridge of her eyeglasses, sweat, slimy and hot, had formed. The glasses slid further down the slope of her nose, and she had pushed them back up, looking at the television set. With her dog Michi at her feet, she heard the noise, the yells—the pulling down of the telephone from the wall. She stretched her arm to the coffee table and grabbed the Rubik's Cube, her eyes no longer following the movement of the cartoon characters on the screen—the colors she wanted to play with already in her hands: white, yellow, red, orange, blue, and green. The Rubik's Cube felt cold to the touch as she swiftly slid each row until order had been found on each of its surfaces—in thirty seconds. Harmony achieved—control.

I was seven, she whispers to herself. The age of reason.

Why don't you still use the cube?

I'm embarrassed by my speed.

The speed at which you complete the cube?

Yes. I think it's because I became a curiosity early on, in school, in class, at home where my parents showed me off. And I didn't like it. People laughed at me, too. I used to wear thick black glasses, you know. Esotropia. Looked like your typical nerd. The cube thing made me look like a perfect one.

Strabismus.

Yes. My eye wandered early on. Funny.

But you do like attracting attention.

Not because of my brains, I don't.

You preferred to rely on your looks.

My brain doesn't gather the men I want around me. The only pleasure I get from them is when I humiliate them. With my brain. And by rejecting them publicly. I'm sure they've became Incels by now.

Because of you.

Yeah. I'm pretty bad.

I see. Going back. The cube had been a source of calm most of your childhood, no?

I guess so.

You've replaced it with what?

Until I hit high school, walking my dog, my rabbit, too, I continued playing with the cube, timing myself in my room.

Once in high school?

Alcohol. Promiscuity.

Were you as sharp with you answer with the other therapists?

Should you ask me such a question? Sounds demeaning. To me. To them, too.

Let me articulate my thought better: I find you quite capable of putting your finger on the right spot. From what you've shared, from before your previous tries. Let's say, I'm impressed.

I know how to impress.

I'm sure you do. And this is not my first rodeo either, Coco.

What a cliché thing to say, Dr. And I'm a good cowgirl?

Coco.

A joke.

Right. Okay. Let's examine your goal. It reads here, in quite perfect calligraphy, I must say, that you want to become a better person. That you want to touch flow.

I think I can do better. Clearly.

You want to?

I think so.

You seem to have a high degree of awareness.

I'd like to stay aware. The problem is that it comes, and it goes. Or sometimes I ignore what it tells me. Then I get in trouble.

What type of trouble?

I already told you. I lose my jobs. It's becoming a problem.

And the letter ...?

I've been trying not to think about it.

Yet, you're here in part because of it.

Life's a paradox.

Give me something, and to yourself, too. I gather you won't tell me who it's from.

Right.

Okay, then. Can you tell me how you felt when you got the letter?

Surprised. Then angry.

Your face shows more sadness than anger.

Maybe. I'd rather move on.

Okay. You losing your job, does it impact the family finances?

No. We have money. But everyone around me is starting to get suspicious. They ask too many questions. I lie about why I don't work. This time around I told Colin, my family as well, that I want to go into philanthropy. Start a foundation.

Do you?

No, sir, I do not.

What were the reasons given before, for you leaving your jobs?

That I was harassed. That the job was below my competencies. That the job was above my competencies. That the boss had fallen in love with me.

All lies.

All lies.

And ... what would a better Coco do? How does she achieve her flow?

Good question ... She doesn't cheat. She forgives and is patient. Has empathy. A better Coco makes a fist but keeps it by her side.

You've given this some thought ... And what does she look like when she has empathy?

She walks tall, her hair in a bun and she wears leather. And she smiles a lot.

Leather?

Yes, why the hell not?

What about the alcohol?

Less alcohol makes Coco a very dull girl.

Dull? Or it pushes awareness away?

If you say so.

Where else has your behavior caused you to suffer?

You see, I'm not sure I suffer so much. Or, using the operative word of the day, I'm *aware* of the impact my flaws have around me. I can understand and see when someone hurts.

But you don't care.

But I don't care. My marriage is okay, considering my wandering eye.

Do you wish to leave your husband?

I don't know ...

As a better Coco, you mentioned nothing about motherhood. The girls, how are you with them?

I think it's the place where I feel the most competent. Where I seem to do little damage. Less damage. With them there is a current I've rarely felt before. I love them. They know it. They love me, too. It's my fuel.

Your parents ...

A sham of a union. My dad was—is still—a philanderer. And my mom, what she flirts with is ... well, craziness.

I understand. Yet, you see a pattern, the same in your life ... you seem to ... How do you reconcile betraying your husband with remaining in your marriage?

I don't, actually. It's the awareness thing, again, you see. I am aware of what I am doing, I just don't care as much as I should. The shame is never there. Or almost …

What do you mean by that? Almost.

I don't think I'm ready to go there.

The letter?

The letter.

All right. This is a perfect place to stop, then. What do you think?

It's always a good place to stop.

Homework.

I figured.

This time, I would like you to find an image, a symbol, a song even—whatever comes to mind—that you think represents you, Coco, as a better person. Bring it to the next session.

A picture of a better me.

In two weeks.

Oh. Why two weeks?

I'm off to a conference in Mexico tomorrow.

What's it about?

Cluster B disorders.

Interesting.

Isn't it.

Well, like I said, Doc, four is my number.

The photo albums are spread on the unmade bed, the bottle of red stands on the night table. Glass in hand, she slowly turns the pages and looks, scrutinizing. It's been twenty years since she last flipped through them, and the same feelings, the same voids. Such obscurity. The photos shine—the black projected by her sight, reflected by her retina. Her and her parents. Cross-country skiing. Snowshoeing. There is a smile on her face, in her eyes, the one eye still wandering, not yet surgically corrected. And then … that picture; that day—a winter picnic, of her beside the snowmobile she had ridden up the skinny trunk of an old black spruce, its needles carpeting the blinding snow. She had mistaken the accelerator for the brakes, climbing up the tree and driving the steering into her stomach. I'm dead! she had screamed. I'm dead! A hearty laugh reaching her, them, so alive in the picture, one could possibly hear it, just looking at it. The smile now is tentative, and she lifts her fingers to the page contouring the image of her sister—Adeline's silhouette. You, she thinks … and she looks up, at her daughter Chloe walking into the bedroom, an open binder in her hand. Okay, she tells her, leave it with me. I'll read it tonight and give you my take on it tomorrow at breakfast.

⸻

How was the trip?

Quite good, thank you. Full, sunny days.

You went alone?

I brought Renée.

Your wife?

Yes.

She's not bored when she goes with you?

Quite the opposite. She's a psychologist.

The power couple, as we say. How long have you been married?

Twenty-two this year.

Children?

Unfortunately, no—

I'm sorry. I was just being curious.

Yes, curiosity, your big resource.

Now you're the one giggling.

Moving on ...

I've researched Cluster B personality disorder sins in the past, before coming here. The other therapists hinted I was a mix of borderline and narcissism.

Then you must know these disorders are the result of trauma that happened to a child before the age of seven. They also don't occur on their own. They blend to form what we call a comorbidity. Rarely have I seen a pure form of anything emerge. A psychiatric single varietal if you will. Labels, Coco, I view them as traps. One has to be careful with them, their use, as it can bring a false sense of security to the table.

Funny. I don't have much memory of anything before twelve.

I see. What's your earliest memory?

Easy. My sister leaving for boarding school.

You never told me you had a sister.

I'm telling you now. And let's leave it at that.

Okay ... Anyhow, labels are just that. A ballpark. An approximation. Perhaps you are many of those, and maybe you are not. Now, let's look at what you brought with you. And a different ending today. We'll finish with a meditation. So, show me.

Well, my process first. I wanted it to be whimsical. My birthday is October 31st ... same as my twins.

Happenstance of some kind. Halloween.

And so, last weekend, I looked at a book Chloe brought home from school. In her English class, they're studying mythologies from other countries. She chose to write about Marzanna, a Slavic figure. And quite the figure.

You identified with her.

I did at first. You see, I love winter, it's my favorite season, and Marzanna, well, she *is* the goddess of winter. And her image—in the book, her hair is black like mine, long and flowing, her eyes, almond-shaped and her lips just as plump. It's me.

Sexy.

Are you even allowed to say that?

I described an image, Coco ... not you. I know the rules.

Right. Anyway, I know it's just an image, made up. Invented. But—

It resonated with you ... what made you change your mind?

I guess I had to go beyond the image. The sorceress. I have the book with me, let me bring it out from my bag ... Listen ... "Marzanna is a destroying fate-goddess who rides the night winds and drinks the blood of men. She is the mare in the word nightmare ..."

That wouldn't flow. Would it?

But wait, there's more. It's also written that as winter approaches, she's associated with, and I quote "[the]enchanted huntsman myth. A tale told by the Roma where a hunter falls in love with Marzanna, and she traps his soul in a magic mirror where he must spend the winter." What would it say of me if I chose her as my symbol?

I don't know. You tell me.

I don't want to be that.

Are you—that?

I think part of me was, is—still. I like to seduce. I like to hurt.

What was her attraction, aside from her so-called attributes?

Her father is the Sun.

Ah.

Run-of-the-mill stuff, but yes. My dad for a while was exactly that. My sun.

And ...

He got remarried. Then I got dropped. We all did.

Dropped? Still?

I'm afraid so. And let's leave the seductress alone. I'm not that dense. I know what you are doing ... So let me show you the image I finally settled on. Here.

You kind of look like her, even more than Marzanna ...

I've been told.

The mysterious Cleopatra.

Her reputation was tarnished through the ages, you know. Unfair. From before she died, the stories written, rewritten, the lack of answers, blanks filled, invented most likely, giving her life this nasty narrative. Rumors carried by time. Orchestrated by men over the ages—even Shakespeare contributed to making her a class-act conniver—always, of course, dissing her. Yes, she had power, had to use it. She was also a mother. A good one, considering the times, and a good leader considering what she had to fight. In essence, they pretty much said she was a bitch. The real deal.

You did your research.

She resonates with me. My narcissistic side? Anyhow, I think she was a decent a bitch.

Decent … How does the image of her bring you closer to feeling a better human?

I'm not sure that is does. All I know is that she was better than me. She was in control, no?

Hum. Until she was killed.

Well, I suppose there's that.

How about you keep looking? Somehow, I think you need to reflect more. And maybe … don't shortchange yourself.

Okay …

You're crying …

It's okay. I'm just tired. The two young ones are sick, and Colin is away.

Would you like to stop here?

No.

Okay, then ... Let's go on. What color do you associate with this fusion of you and this image?

Purple.

The scent.

Burning coal.

The music.

Let me think for a minute ... No. Nothing is coming. Maybe by the next session? And with a new image ...

Yes, and yes.

The homework?

Maybe an easier one, this time around. I was thinking, you bring your girls to the park, no? Next time you do, observe specifically what it is you see in them, what part of them is you, what part is not you, and that you would like to have.

A walk in the park ...

Funny ... Maybe. All right, then, Coco. We have ten minutes before the session is over.

Meditation time.

Yes. We'll be doing some traveling.

Dr. Rubenstein, some place cold, please.

I'm happy to see you. I was worried a little. You cancelled the last three sessions.

I respected the cancellation policy.

And I thank you for that. How are you?

Colin left me.

Sit down, Coco ...

Okay ... He found out. Someone from the office called him. Bound to happen.

How do you feel?

Colin? Jaded, to tell you the truth—relieved? He decided to travel for the year.

What about the girls?

We decided not to tell them anything other than Daddy has a big contract up north and that he'll be gone for a while. There's no need in messing up the start of school.

It makes sense.

All this happened the same time I took Cara and Marianne to the park.

And?

It's Marianne. She fell off the monkey bars. A belly flop, right there on the sand. And somehow, I couldn't catch her in time. I was right there. The weight of her fall ... her face was pushed in glass buried just under the surface. Broken beer bottles.

I'm sorry.

But there's more ... Something similar happened to Adeline.

Adeline ...?

My sister.

I see.

I've never told anyone the story.

I understand.

While up north, where we lived, our dog, Michi, her puppies—they were about two months old, seven big, plump, furry puppies. She was half-wolf and half-collie, I think. A bit like me now that I think of it ... Your smiling

...

I'm smiling because this analogy coming from your mouth is coherent with the view you have of yourself. No?

I'd like to be more wolf to tell you the truth.

Another one.

And you smile, still.

Yes. Go on.

We wanted to play with them. I'm seven, she's twelve. The crate was in an awkward space, difficult to access, wedged between the sofa, my father's stereo system, and a wall. I watched her bend to retrieve a puppy. She turned around and squeezed passed me just before where the stereo furniture was standing. Then she fell. Headfirst.

Her face on the glass shelves where Dad placed his records. All four shelves. Broken.

And your daughter?

Yes. They both wear the same scar now. On the same cheek. A three-inch Harry Potter scar. That's what I tell Marianne. Fortunately, unlike Adeline, Marianne's forehead was spared.

What do you make of that?

The forehead?

No. The similarities.

Well for starters, Marianne is not as pretty—striking?—as my other girls. She's often teased about it, too. Makes me sad. For the rest, it triggered some memories. Not the best ones.

How is Marianne?

I think she will be fine. She cried a lot when we removed the sutures, she was afraid of what she'd see. But I think the scar will be more discreet than Adeline's. Finer. I said that we'll go have it fixed if it doesn't heal well. Showed her images of models who had scars. It quieted her. At the doctor's office, I remembered how Adeline's wound was sutured in a makeshift hospital. She had to wait twenty-four hours before they got to her face, you know. One whole day. The only doctor on site was away on an emergency. A construction accident. Not a plastic surgeon, either. My sister's scar never quite healed. Rosacea got into it. Then it made a thick flap on her cheek.

You've seen your sister since then? Didn't the sight of the scar remind you of anything?

Never. Everything came rushing back when Marianne fell.

Hum. How did your sister handle the accident? Do you remember?

Yes , I had time to untangle the day's images. She was quite composed, in the moment. It happened so fast she never felt the cuts. It was Mom that stirred the pot. It's quite vivid in my mind, now. She kept yelling that Adeline would never look the same again. That she was disfigured. That's when I remember her starting to cry. And when Marianne raised her face to me, the image of Adeline bringing her fingers to her cheek popped in my head. I saw her look at the blood on her fingers. I heard her cries mingle with those of Marianne's.

Okay. So, an accident.

That was never Adeline's story, though. She said I tripped her. I think that that was when I blocked everything from my head.

Your heart, too ... Did you, trip her?

I don't know. I did feel my feet on her leg. That's all I remember.

How were the two of you in general, then?

She was a stranger to me. She never looked at me. She never did anything with me. I was invisible to her.

Did you want to be visible?

I think that I did. Looking back, I'm pretty sure I didn't want to be a stranger to her. I can see that now. That I wanted her in my life. It's all coming back to me in a very stroboscopic kind of way, if you will.

I see.

Your dad in all this?

Mom called Dad, in a panic. He came rushing back and brought Adeline to the hospital.

What was your initial reaction to the whole incident?

I felt gleeful.

And today?

I don't know.

You're leaving. We still have twenty minutes.

I need to go.

<hr>

The place is noisy, the glass full—a California Merlot. Three hours of sitting at the bar, her fingers tapping to the sound of the barman's whistling. She looks around and she doesn't see much, and then, the music, Personal Jesus,

Johnny Cash's version. I should bring this to Rubenstein. A good laugh.

Her head tilted, she travels back to that day, the park—before the event. Marianne is nothing like me, she thinks. Shy. Introverted. Generous. And Chloe and Josephine, they want a stage to live on, a place from which they can pull people to. Definitely more me. And Cara, she's all Colin, sports and books. And who would I want to be like—more?

Another bottle and now, the blur is upped, vaguer. She only sees when she closes her eyes, letting her lids fall into place—her daughters; asking; probing. Some form of clarity emerging, and when she touches it, she loses her balance, falls from her high-stool. Marianne—Adeline. Yes. It's time to go, Miss. She feels the hand pulling her, and she unfolds, looking at him. You know, Barry, I've never met a man who whistled because he was happy. They're either sad, or about to hit.

A sound meant to pull the wool over our eyes.

———

How long have you two been estranged?

Twenty years.

What happened?

She found out I hit on her husband.

Is it true?

Yes.

Why did you do it?

Because I could, why else? Because back then I thought she had too much of everything I didn't have. Money. Success. Beautiful kids. Jealousy of the very common kind.

How did she find out?

Five years into their marriage and he told her when they had a fight.

Did you expect him to keep it a secret?

All I did was take his hand toward their bedroom. The guests' coats were there. It was Christmas time. A party. I told him I needed help finding my wallet.

Strategic ambiguity.

Yet he understood my intent. And he was right.

Do you miss her?

Hard to say. Miss what? We didn't have much. Never did anything together. With our parents, either. No family activities. A big void.

Do you want to fill it?

What if I like voids?

You wouldn't be here if you did.

Touché.

Reviewing my notes, Coco, I couldn't help but notice—about your mother. You say you kept in touch with her whereas Adeline never did? Why is that?

Right. Mom was never well, as I explained to you. She was often compared to Joan Crawford—Mommy Dearest. When she wasn't doing well, when she came back from her hospital stays, the only one she wanted to see was Adeline. Adeline Adeline Adeline. Mom was like a leech, and one day, Adeline had had enough of it and told her to fuck off. It was then, Mom turned to me. I became her new thing to latch on to. But in all fairness, it was easy to tolerate. She's now had Alzheimer's for some time—and she's forgotten about Adeline and became quite endeared by me. It's a good form of crazy now. Palatable. She's even developed quite a sense of humor.

A new mother.

I guess so.

Did you finish reading your sister's memoir?

I'm on page 267.

And?

And we'll see.

They walk the streets dragging the leaves with their feet, yet the walk is fast—excited. Around them, the sound of an anticipated night finally arriving, and they walk through it with laughter, for levity's hour has stoked their time, now. When she turns around, Coco observes her daughters climbing the porch stairs, a pillowcase in each of their hands, half-full. More candies dropped into their cases, and they walk back to her, with wide chocolate-smeared smiles on their faces. What a troupe we make, Cara says, we outdid ourselves this Halloween, and turning to Marianne, she takes a lipstick from her pant pocket and paints her little sister's lips a brighter pink. This is the best, she tells her, your costume. You like it? Marianne asks. How can I not, you silly goose.

You're Kelly Mitchell—the queen of gypsies.

You know what today is?

I'm well aware of it, sir. Look at me.

I noticed when you walked in. Leather pants and hair in a bun.

Yes. The outfit to highlight it's been two years. What do you think?

A very good way to anchor it. And it was empathy, I recall.

Let's just say, I'm more aware now, and more often, and it stays with me longer. Thank you, Dr. Rubenstein.

And thank you, for trusting me. My process. I was wondering before you came in, do you think we're approaching the end of our time together?

I thought of it, too. Not sure about that. I have a new job I'd like to keep, as you know. The head of small pension fund. Employees to manage. I've reduced my drinking. So … And Colin and I are thinking of patching things up, too. I may need a little of your presence before I fly solo, for a while anyway.

Understood. I'm always here … You finally brought me an image, I see … It makes me happy …

Yes, yes, here. We were browsing a little boutique down in the art district. The moment I walked in, it struck at me.

It's not a typical portrait this time.

No. I don't feel the need anymore. Another type of beauty …

A Spanish artist.

Salvadorian—Fernando Llort. Elevo Mi Alma.

I lift my soul.

You know Spanish.

I do.

I love the colors. I love the woman depicted. Her crown like a hat. She could be a jester, too. Her large body. Her arms, like she's holding the world. Me. I feel safe when I look at her. And I do want to lift it, you know. My soul.

You feel ... lighter?

And better about myself ... I never thought that I would, touch it, you know, the feeling ... I have a gift for you, Dr. Rubenstein.

Oh! An envelope. I gather—the famous letter?

Yes. The famous letter. Here.

You want me to read it now?

If it's okay with you. She's divorced now, by the way. Lost everything. But she's doing what she loves ...

She writes?

Yes. And quite well.

***

The windshield wipers toss the snow, the speed of them slow, the sound, gentle and lulling. The car is parked a block away from the apartment building, close enough for Coco to see.

The distance—safe.

Yet.

I can't Colin, I want to go back home. I'm not sure about this anymore. What if ...

She's there waiting for you, in this storm, Coco. Just look at her. One shot, that's it. If it doesn't work, we'll come back another day. Or maybe we won't. But you made it this far. You worked on this.

She closes her eyes, grips the handle, and her feet push the car door into the small snowbank bordering the sidewalks. Squeezing herself from the narrow space, she loses her footing and stumbles to the ground. Her eyes meet Colin's, telling him she thinks this is an omen, that they should go. He smiles as he shakes his head, no, a soft and loving, no. She stands, immobile, watching Adeline wait for her, head to the sky with hands ungloved, catching the snow; its flakes, plump, their fall, a tranquil flow.

She walks a stealth walk, knowing of herself, knowing of why, of this moment, a crafted one, one she has never dreamt about, until now. And now it was here, her sister sitting on the steps of the building wrapped in a fur coat she's seen before. Inside another north.

Hey.

Adeline turns to her and stands. I didn't think you'd come.

To tell you the truth, I almost didn't.

You haven't changed. Just as beautiful. She paused, staring. Your eyes, too, so luminous.

You're mistaken, Adeline.

I suppose you have changed.

I think I have.

Me too, you know. Didn't have much choice …

Adeline turns her body to the building's entrance, and looking away, she feels the seconds that precede all things made of hope; of love. She looks back at her sister, smiles. Frankly, Coco, I've had enough of the cold. Come inside, I've prepared coffee, that and your favorite dessert.

A Brittany cake?

A Brittany cake.

How did you know?

Coco—I never didn't know.

The A Side

MUSIC HAD ALWAYS PADDED their cell. Their home. Music sometimes burying, sometimes amplifying, tones, words. Cries. Music, his gift to her. And music wasn't playing in her head as they glided down the ski hill, the strong silhouette ahead of her. There was no need for a buffer. Not then. He was there, the laughter from his chest, a sound made of her.

The transgression that would never become.

She looked at him, her father, the sun seeming reachable to her, low, a cold yellow shining on the slope's white powder. There are moments meant to be captured, she would think later when revisiting this one and realizing it could have never been different. Or more—because of nature's law. Where nothing that precedes or follows a moment such as this one, matters—a silo unable to leak its goodness into the past or future, however much one wishes it to be so.

It would be dangerous, anyway, for this type of goodness to leak out.

No one on the small hill, the skiers having left the cold; the T-bar pulling them to the top; the constant sound of skis kissing the soft-packed snow. They said nothing, Brodeur, a lit cigarette in his mouth; Adeline, looking straight ahead and seeing more shades of yellow stringing through the clouds. The last run was on their minds. Adeline had lost her balance, and her father not far behind, unable to avoid her, had gently collided with her from behind, pushing her into the forest. The drift into the edge of the wood had lasted thirty seconds. A long thirty seconds, replete with peace. Replete with more. Leftovers, too.

At the end of the day as they walked to the truck, the sun was still shining, yet a storm coming to her.

The cell.

She retreated inside the sounds he had chosen to play from his Sony reel-to-reel—it was louder than usual, as she walked to her bedroom. Once inside, she walked on the dozens of vinyl records carpeting the floor and sat on the wicker chair, having tossed the mountain of clothes off the seat and onto the floor. His music was not buffering anything anymore—Eva had lost it, again—and agitated, Adeline stood, walked to the sound system her father had given to her the year before, slowly placing her head inside the chunky, leather-made headset.

The Dark Side of The Moon. Time.

So much of time ahead and waiting for her—wasted time and fruitful darkness coming from so many sides—wise men will try to convince, pushing lulling narratives. And she will sink into time's hole, swallowed by the illusion of an abundance accessible to her. To her only.

She walked to her bed and pulled the long cord from the amplifier, sliding underneath the thin, down-filled blanket, her back to the mattress. She closed her eyes. Behind them, waves of light sprang. Sunny things, her friends, undulating inside her brain.

This time—that day, Adeline Brodeur will visit millions of times, a crutch more than a push, to remember; convince herself that she was loved, that she was seen. If only one time.

That time.

And she will whisper to herself, when alone, when unpacking life's funky little handouts, inflating their meaning, their essence, gaslighting herself: Thank you, Father.

Because—the music.

Cold Chaos

The summer rain drops hard on the roof—water knocking at her mind, intruding on her thoughts; of leaving; of staying; of never forgetting.

This place.

I'm alone here. The last one left.

Her back to the mattress, she twists her head, toward the window, and she sees the moon, its glitter glittering. The moon lives here, with me. The cold cold of the moon with the cold cold of my land.

My summer's land. The ending of my last summer.

The ticking of the clock mingles with the tickling of thoughts on a mind that is too porous. Fragile. Set on the floor, tilted toward her, the clock's face is looking at her, its needles threading sand, and she looks at the vert-de-gris colored teller of obscurity's time. 3:00 a.m.

Her throat constricts and as it does, she recalls the empty space that is the space she has lived in for the last three months. The last ten years. The house emptied of all that had been a home, a modest home, and gone now to sink into a city's insanity—the insane demands on the minds of those wanting lichen-laced ground; dancing night firmaments; snowbanks that frame the lives of all things called solitude. I am a solitary, she thinks, of the snow-worshipping kind. A worshipper of cold solitude.

Her head is pounding, and she feels pain's fingers threaten to reach more of her insides. I need to move, she thinks, shake it out. And so, she straightens, the terrycloth robe she fell asleep in, loosely cinched at the hip, and walking to the bedroom door, she thinks of today. The last return reachable, yet not wanting to be fully reached.

And still no signs of him.

A walk in the corridor—the sight of her sister's empty room—a cold prayer to a shadow tethered to her flawed flesh and bones: I cannot pour any of your blood out of mine, I cannot fight it, this line, bitterness as a failed genesis. I don't have a choice, Coco. I have all the reasons in the world to hate you; all the reasons in the world to shut you out from my head, and my guts, and yes, my heart, and yet I do think of you—I love you beyond unconditionality's dictums. And I don't understand why I do. The reasons, nonexistent.

Tears should roll, but they do not, instead, the rising of a certitude called Mother, a human regulated by vanity's claws; craziness's long and hard touch. Her turn: I do wish you could have been someone else, she whispers to her absence. But as I will become—grow older, you too, will stay with me, your own features moving, penetrating my face. In the mirror we will melt, Mother, at least, with the parts of you I can understand.

Reaching the living room, she walks to the sound system, the only furniture her father allowed her to keep. It will keep you company during the summer, he said. It did.

She kneels to it, presses the power button, and she lies down, her head to the speaker—music, a strong wind coming to her cheek. She listens, eyes shifting, to the roll playing out her years, end-to-end melodies of her, about her.

Waking up, Adeline stands and faces the living room window, a wide, clear early morning brushing the inside of the space she stills in. Moving slowly, she walks to the kitchen, and looking up, she sees the plane ticket placed at the top of the refrigerator. She picks it up, puts it on the kitchen counter, near the stove. She walks to the suitcase butterflied across the kitchen floor—a suitcase almost brimming; a suitcase waiting to be closed.

She gets dressed, slipping into real summer clothes—a beige sleeveless and flowery dress—clothes meant for the city; clothes the cold and rainy weather hasn't allowed her to wear during the whole of her gig as the manager of the only bait shop at the camp, the place where workers living in simply furnished dormitories could access a safe and reliable area to store their catch before returning home. A smile forms, the sight of the large communal freezer's inside, a man's treasure chest, coming to mind, its tall steel shelves packed from bottom to top with fish: trout, brown and speckled and red, pike, salmon, walleye, wrapped in newspaper, a numbered tag hanging from their tail. Often enough, a frozen fish had fallen on her head as she retrieved a client's loot from its high placement. You should wear a hard hat when you're in here, they all said each time a fall had occurred.

She smiled.

At first, the workers had been skeptical of her, this teenage girl managing a man's world. But word had gotten around: this girl knew her rods, her reels, her lures, the test of lines; and she knew about the rivers, understood the currents, the behavior of fish. The men had seen her passion for this place, the wildness in her tamed by the land's own.

Her mind became lighter. Yes, she thought, turning the inside of her hand toward her and looking at her palm—an unsutured wound from a lure that had hooked itself in the fleshy part of her hand as she was cleaning the office. And she thought of Quinn. Soft-spoken Quinn O'Donnell, the son of Hugh O'Donnell, her father's right-hand man. The crush that had remained one.

Where are you?

Like most of the men working the job site, Quinn's schedule was a grueling one, with only Sundays providing time for rest. Time with her, at the end of her Sunday shifts.

The first time he walked into the shop, the connection had been facile, flowing through their laughing eyes—a constant current. This awareness of who they both were—an immediate recognition, as if they understood the magnitude of the coincidence; as if they once were brother and sister, he often liked to say, adding that maybe in the Middle Ages, maybe they had been. Brother. Sister. His words, at first, she had ignored, convinced shyness was to blame—who wants to date a sibling? Shyness and his strict upbringing. There was nothing Irish about him. He didn't drink; he didn't fight; he never swore. He wants to take his time, she had thought.

For the first three weeks following their first encounter, following the end of her workday, he picked her up to go fishing near the closest dam. KA3. A third Sunday came, and as they rode back to her house for a simple dinner of floured speckled trout and French fries—a picnic style dinner held in the middle of the living room—she became silent, the gravel flying onto the truck, the only sound coming to them. The word sister was running inside her head.

Back at her house that night, while each sat on a tall speaker, a paper plate perched on their knee, they spoke about the day's fishing, about the lures she chose—her patience, too. I don't know how you do it, Adeline Brodeur, but you sure know how to pull the fish from the water. With you, it's like shooting them in a barrel. Smiling, she mumbled a quick response, suddenly feeling tired. Nothing to it, really. Go at dawn. Go at dusk, like we do. Understand where they feed, and love to fish in the rain—everybody knows that. And yeah, here we fish in a barrel, a huge one, Quinn, there's so many fish in these waters to make Glaucus redundant.

Glaucus?

She shook her head and laughed. All this European education and you don't know? She took a bite of her food and with a mouthful explained Glaucus was the entity protecting fishermen. We don't need him around here, Quinn. All of us are God-like on these waters. Half-human. Half-Glaucus.

Like all the other Sunday nights before, he returned to his dorm, thanking Adeline, and brushing a kiss on her cheek. And each time, her heart sunk. She was falling in love. A first love, expecting it to be requited.

While the hydro project was nearing its conclusion, with workers let go and structures dismantled—housings, dormitories, cultural and sporting facilities—the Red Caribou Lounge had remained open every night of the week. A spirit booster for the ones left to witness the end of their lives as neopioneers.

Inside the walls of this trailer disguised as a small discotheque, once or twice during the week, they met, candidly sharing about their pasts and their futures; about their fears; about their falls. One night, amidst the thinning crowd of patrons, both sitting at the bar, she invited Quinn to finish the night at her house. You'll sleep better, she told him with beaming eyes. I will, too. Without a word, and holding hands, they left the premises, indifferent to the eyes of the men who envied them—him mostly.

On the road, the car sliced into the dusk to Adeline's house. At the wheel, just like hers, Quinn's demeanor became looser, and with Adeline's hand still in his, the union of their fingers resting between each their seat, he listened to her retell the stories of fish and the men chasing them. They all ring true, she said. Yet I know they lie, just like they must lie about the size of their dicks, she said, smiling, surprised as he was at her capacity to banter. But the funniest one, this one a true story, she added, shaking her head, was when my uncle came to visit us, two years ago. A fishing trip. It had been a generous one, and when he returned, packing his frozen catches inside cardboard boxes, Dad played a trick on him. As my uncle waited in line to board the plane, Dad, being Jean Brodeur and all, stepped inside the airport manager's office, at the back of the counter. There, he wrapped and scotch-taped images of Playboy centrefolds around the boxes. She paused, placing a hand over her mouth, unable to contain the giggles. Apparently, once arriving at the airport in Montreal, Dorval, my uncle waited for his box to slide down the belt onto the luggage carousel, laughing with the other passengers at the breast and hairy crotch clad box waiting to be picked up.

He was the last one standing?

Yes, he was, she said, as she shook her head more.

You miss your dad? Quinn suddenly asked.

Adeline became serious. I do, and I don't. It's complicated. Awkward since he's remarried. You?

I miss him until I'm with him. Then, when I'm with him, I don't understand what it was I missed.

He's the one running the place now since my dad left. The workers seem to like him ...

Well, you know what they say about treating strangers better than family ...

Adeline removed her hands from his grip. I only know about being replaced, she thought to herself, and by a stranger that will remain one. We're almost there Quinn, she said, pointing to her house.

The night had completely fallen by the time they stood at the front door. She took her keys from her coat pocket, and as she tried to unlock the door, her hands started to shake. Gently, Quinn placed his hands over hers, guiding it until the lock clicked. Inside her head, a blank; far inside her mouth, the feel of her throat narrowing. They stepped inside the house, and without saying a word, they walked to the end of the corridor, to where her bedroom was. At the doorway, they stilled. He pointed at her hands, smiled a crooked smile. Your first time?

She considered him, his question, and she looked at him, a long look, pregnant with hesitation. Do all truths need to be told? Shared? Does rape count as a first time? she let out.

Quinn's left eyelid started to flutter. What do you mean?

Silent, she took his hand and pulled him inside the bedroom.

Remaining dressed, they stood, the light from the lamp posts along the utilidors the only real clarity reaching the moment.

I'm so sorry, he said.

I know. I am, too.

Who knows?

Only you, now. She latched on to his gaze and smiled. I'm okay though, somehow. I just don't think about it so much. Her eyes fell on her hands. I think it was me—

Your hands ...

Yes. I know. I guess shame makes them shake.

Here, he said as he pressed her to sit on the bed. We both need to rest. Tomorrow is Wednesday, I have to work ...

I don't start until noon ...

The main thing is we don't have to do anything ... Shouldn't, maybe ...?

Remaining dressed and lying on the bed close to him, her head on his chest, she finally shared her secret: the party; the neglected door, left ajar; the emergency landing. Quinn listened, the disquiet in his heart known to his senses, weighty, and seemingly understanding the severity of the wound. Inside the moment's silence, they remained awake, hands holding hands, hands holding hearts. The obscurity was lifting, the white light sifted by the low line of clouds coming through the large window. Morning. And when he stood, Adeline, now asleep, he pulled the scrunched-up bed cover from the floor and covered her small body with it. He stayed for a while, his gaze hovering, scanning even. Her body, the hint of it under the covers, he could guess: the small curves, the small waist, her long thin legs. His eyes running along her legs to where her bare feet hung, exposed, he smiled at the size of them. So big for such a delicate frame, he thought, directing his attention to her face; this sleeping face, a mouth half-open, made of full and reddish lips, inviting lips, lush eye lashes curling over her lids, a nose, noticeable yet a feature belonging to the rest of her facial intricacies. All of her. Tears came. Expected tears coming from a known well. I will call you, he said, placing a kiss on her hand.

I promise.

It had been two weeks since then, and Quinn had disappeared.

Time had gone.

Time had come to leave everything behind. To leave the density of all her memories inside a ground that would hold them forever, inside its cold. A cold that keeps. A cold that prevents the rot from invading matters that matter.

She shakes her head as she wipes the wet from the rim of her eyes. It's over, she thinks.

Her movements are brusque, harsh even this time around, as if the body understands before the mind that the best way to exit is to disappear from this place. Quickly. Scanning the surface of her dress with her hands, she knows shivers will travel with her to the airport, and so, she places a parka over her shoulders. It will keep me warm, she thinks, until I take my seat at the front of the plane.

She closes the suitcase, props herself on the kitchen counter, and looks to the window. Ahead, she sees a portion of the neighbor's house. The family of five that left the week before, one week after the departure of their container for a destination she ignores. The Canadian Maritimes, she thinks, that or somewhere in northern California. The pre-manufactured house is being dismembered—hers is set to be, too, in four days—as the trailer waits for the two modules to be loaded onto its flatbed. The sound of a horn comes. Ah, she says to herself, my ride. The last ride. Her boss. Flying off the counter, she grabs her suitcase, and walking toward the door, she can feel a fight emerging inside her head, its conclusion as well. A lump forms in her chest. When she steps outside, the wind is dead, the sun is beaming and the men working on the neighbor's house are whistling a tune she can't recognize. She nods to them, and she descends the stair to the sedan. When she takes her seat, she doesn't say a word. The man at the wheel doesn't either.

The road to the airport, her heart can recite. Like a poem. There will be the last house located at the edge of the main road leading away from the village; first to the camp, then farther north, to the airport. A thirty-minute ride, yet it will flash as if anesthesia had been needled into her veins, accelerating time, depriving her of the now.

Adeline, she hears. Adeline. Time to go.

She opens her eyes. They have arrived. Yes. Yes, I know. It's time to go. She opens the door. And thank you for the ride.

Good luck, he says, with your studies, and all. He reaches into his coat pocket and removes an envelope. Your bonus.

She nods and as she does, she grabs her luggage, places the envelope inside her bag. Yes, she thinks. Thank you.

The walk to the airport counter feels as though she is walking through a sludge. The voices, all male, are distorted to her ears, still she manages to hear her name being called, and repeated. She can hear the snarky in their tone. She doesn't care; no—she likes it. To be known. Somewhere, if just here, now.

She checks in and takes her seat just as boarding is called out.

When the doors leading outside to the tarmac open, she takes her place in the queue. The men's walk to the air stairs is brisk, purposeful. They want to flee to their women and their families. Or nothing that resembles this place. She tries to keep up with the man ahead of her, but her legs, suddenly becoming numb and stiff, won't obey. A push. Faster, the man behind her says. Move, Brodeur. The push startles her and she falls, her knees and hands to the hard-packed gravel. Pebbles and sand have lodged in the palms, mixing with her blood. The man apologizes, helps her to her feet, then continues to the plane. That's when she hears her name being called out. A choir to her ears. She turns to the voices, lets the other passengers walk past her. The reveal feels gradual to her eyes: Six men are gathered fifty meters from where she stands and looking at her. Her eyes zoom in. She knows all of them. They were her favorite clients. Her summer. And there, too, Quinn. Her eyes swell, and she cannot contain the surge. The tallest, he walks to her, leading the others to do the same. In his hands, a rectangular box, and on his face, a wide smile is spreading. Miss, she hears from behind. She turns around, sees the flight attendant waving her in. We are waiting for you. Speechless, she turns back to the men, toward him, brushes the dirt from her palms—a mindless gesture. Here, he says, I thought you'd want this, Adeline, as a souvenir. He hands her the shoe-like box. He looks beyond Adeline, to the flight attendant fidgeting at the top of the air-stairs. You gotta go now, Miss Brodeur, says one of the men. There's nothing more to see here, for we took it all. And thank you.

Goodbyes echo to her, and she watches the men turn around; watches their gait, slow and fast; watches checkered coats and blue uniforms walk into the wind—his back is shrinking, too, the distance the enemy. She looks up, her tears settling mid-cheek. The sky has become covered by a stretch of gray. It's too early for snow, yet she knows all is possible. That nothing has never not be seen, here on this land.

The walk is abrupt. So is the climb to the open door. She ignores the flight attendant's words, short and dry, and she walks to the second row. Both seats are free, and she sits by the window, placing the box on her knees, then sliding it underneath the seat before her. Inside the plane, cigarette smoke is floating, and the noise is deafening, the laughter of its passengers, obnoxious.

The door is safely closed. The fasten your seatbelt sign comes on. The safety reminders quickly administered. The two flight attendants take to their seats.

Fastening her seat belt, Adeline looks out the porthole, feels the wheels rolling to one end of the landing strip, sees the world slowly moving, too. When the plane stills, she does as well, the anticipation loaded inside her belly. Somehow, this time, she doesn't feel the need to count background until the plane is safe in the air. In the distance, through the porthole she sees Quinn's truck slowly rolling off the airport parking lot. What happened, she wonders as the engines open. The plane is launched, and a smile comes, sudden, healing—she remembers Michi breaking free from the rope tethering her to the house's porch; Michi spotted running along the tarmac as a plane was taking off; Michi, now gone, mauled by a bear. Still, she smiles. The death had been a fitting one for this half-wild thing. An apropos death. I hope it will be the same for me, just as fitting, she surprises herself thinking.

Her eyes to the running earth, she feels the plane become airborne. The ascent is slow, unsteady, rattled by the winds. Looking down, trees—the sticks of life, standing on shallow soil, married to the water surrounding them form a sparsely spread forest. More altitude is gained, and when the plane veers to the left, hovering high over the Caniapiscau River, a known makeshift landing strip materializes before her. The Galina strip. She wants to smile but she can't. Just then, the sound of a bell, followed by the captain's voice. A bit of turbulence, he says. Keep your seatbelts on. Arrival time at destination is on cue.

One hour into the flight, holding a plastic glass filled with rum and Coke, she brings the tray next to her seat down, and places the drink on it. From underneath her seat, she retrieves the box, places it on her lap. Before untying the twine, she shakes the box the way she would at

Christmas when little—the guesses always wrong. She tilts the box from side to side, feels a hard weight hitting the sides of the box. It makes her smile.

She undoes the twine and unwraps the box. When she removes the lid, her smile morphs into a high pitch chuckle. She takes the small but elongated package in her hands. Wrapped in newspaper, the gift is still cold, still hard, and a small envelope has been rolled around its end. Of course, she whispers to herself. She tries to unroll the envelope from what she knows is the tail end of a fish, but the tape keeping it in place won't give in, and so she presses on the service button above her head. A knife please, she asks the flight attendant. It takes two minutes and finally the envelope is freed, its content as well.

His handwriting, she sees for the first time. Neat, constant—an engineer's reliability. She swallows and reads.

Adeline,

I will be leaving this place soon and will never come back. Like you. I think we both know no one but us, those who have lived here, however short the time we stayed, can understand the span and depth of our complicated adventure that was this land that should had never been found. Solitude bordering loneliness. The cold of the land leading to the warmth of men. At times. Isolation tamed by the presence of silence. And you have made a difference for me, you brought me some hope, little one. Light, luminosity. For I, too, have a past, a recent one. I never told you. The death of my only sibling, my sister Kathleen, two years ago. A rape. A murder. Will you understand? When you shared your story, I couldn't do anything, let alone give you what I knew you needed. What I wanted to. I couldn't be the first one. The real first one. And so, while thinking of you, our stories, over the last two weeks, I made you this while on my breaks. You'll see, I am not too bad at welding ... but I'm not so sure it is my calling, either. Will you wear it, please when you think of me?

And smile.

I have missed you. I will miss you. Maybe someday ...?

I hope you forgive me, my Duchess.

Please. Forgive me.

Quinn.

She places the letter on her tray and looks inside the box. At the bottom lies another package. How did I miss that, she wonders. This time, the smaller gift is wrapped inside wrinkled silk paper, white and glittery. She picks it up assessing the weight, her fingers stopping at the edge of something she cannot guess. When the inside of her hands starts to pound, as if the wound had suddenly grown a heart, she places the unknown object on the seat beside her and she closes her eyes and caresses her hand with her thumb. Quinn's face appears, the tasting of his lips by the river, near the dam—the slow lifting of the green mesh protecting her face from the clouds of black flies hovering over their heads. The first kiss. The only kiss. Through her closed lids, tears finally come, unweaving an array of confusions.

The shuffle of feet, a voice feminine and soft. Is everything all right, Miss? If there is anything I can do …

Adeline opens her eyes, shakes her head. No, thank you. All is fine. She turns her attention to the seat beside her, retrieving the unwrapped object. Delicately, she undoes the random folds, slowly ripping the tape from the paper, stiff and crisp. Gradually, she reveals the item, and when she sees what it is, she laughs. A diadem. An improvised diadem, its filigree incomplete, its low peaks adorned with what she can only assume are plastic green beads. Green. Like your eyes, she can hear him say. Like Ireland.

The captain's voice comes onto the circuit. We are starting our descent. The flight is on time, and we should be at the gate by 7:30 p.m.

Adeline checks her watch. 6:55 p.m. She knows the drill, to secure her tray, straighten her seat, and fasten her seat belt. She places the wrapped fish in the box, the box underneath the seat in front of her. And as the plane descends, she looks out the porthole. The sun is still alive. Below, signs of civilization materialize.

The wheels hit the ground. The plane wobbles. A steady roll to the gate. Eyes wide open, Adeline remains seated until the last man deplanes.

When she sees all passengers have disembarked, she stands, straightens her dress and slips her bag across her body. Box in hand, she wiggles away from her seat. As she walks the few steps to where the crew has gathered at the front of the plane, she can feel heat coming from outside reaching her. Hot heat. The scent of the vapor escaping the tarmac, too. It is harsh. A reminder of this other land's existence, its own mines waiting for her. A recalibration of her senses, and the messages they carry flood her nerve pathways; a chokehold of certainties form around her throat. He is gone. They all have left her.

People don't stay, she now knows.

She passes by the crew, mouths a thank you, and steps onto the air-stairs' landing. Grabbing the rail with one hand, she stills. The wind is gone. More heat and sweat are painting her face. Mother is waiting, she apprehends. So, is Coco. Of course, not Dad. She turns back, a hand securing the tiara now perched on her head. The flight attendant returns her smile. It is just as weak. You don't have a choice, she says. None of us do.

The vast space inside Adeline's mind starts to shrink, and she returns the stare, one blanked by memory that will soon return to the soil it was born from. She squints to the woman, her right eye fluttering, and she wonders less about the time she is leaving behind. Turning her body to the sunlight, she descends the stairs, feeling lost nor found to this moment, the sense of a barbed wire stretching from her heel to the top of her head, the weaving of a twisted stability she will have to chase most of her life. I wonder, she thinks more, walking the tarmac, if this woman knows about a Duchess' fate. Better yet, about the fate awaiting a sad and lonely Queen. So many deaths, she whispers to no one, have carpeted the stone-cold floors of the most insane of kingdoms.

Never one too many.

Now.

The McGill auditorium was full, 200 students like me. I sat at the back—the nosebleeds. My first class since the abortion that had halted my freshman year two years before—a drunken encounter in a bar—since my return from up north. I felt scared. I felt apprehensive. I was living with Dad and his new wife, and Coco, as well. Commuting with him every morning and night, the suburb to down-town, the ride eloquent with awkward silence. A messy silence.

I left the Sociology of Work class having understood nothing, the professor's thick British accent too much for my French-fed brain to untangle. I watched the students hurry to their next destination, and I wondered about mine. My next class was at 3:00 p.m. My watch told me it was 11:00 a.m.

I decided to sit on the stairs of the Arts building and smoke it out, a book in hand. It was a hot September day, and I should have felt the warmth of it on my skin, yet I was shivering. It was then, as I took a long drag from my stick, that I heard her voice.

Hey. You picked up smoking, I see.

I looked up and saw her standing and smiling at me, stunned as much as I was, her face so gaunt.

She sat beside me, pointing ahead. I'm just passing through. My boyfriend plays for the football's Redmen, and I promised him I'd meet him after practice, outside the stadium.

She took a cigarette pack from her purse, lighting one up, and we remained still, quiet—fifteen minutes of blowing out smoke.

I was the one who broke the silence. Majoring in Industrial Relations, I said, staring at her. First day. Real one, I thought.

Me, I've decided to travel the world. Not sure still what I'll be studying. Just came back from visiting Vietnam and southern China.

Nice. I'm curious. Did you ever go back?

No. Never did.

Your boyfriend …

He's from British Columbia. An engineering student. Met him during a layover in Beijing.

Right.

It's been a while … Adeline …

Yes, it has, I said, wringing my hands.

What happened, she asked softly, pointing at my hands. Your fingers are so white. Dead-white.

Well, you know, Charlotte, I laughed, surprise, surprise. They can't warm up, it seems. My toes and my nose. The same. Raynaud's disease. Since I've been back.

You can't warm up?

It's intermittent. I became allergic to the cold, the doctor tells me. Any change in the weather triggers an episode.

But it's so warm today …

They say too much accumulated shit does the deed, too… Chaos, I whispered.

Oh … How do you treat that?

Funny thing. Sometimes, cold water does the trick for me.

Go figure.

I know.

She pinched my waist, lifting a portion of my blouse. You gained weight …

Not so much, I think … but you …

Arms to her chest, tucking her stomach inside her large sweatshirt, she smiled a triumphant smile. I'm fine, she said. Don't worry.

I stood, looked at my watch. Your boyfriend can wait, Charlotte, so get up. I've got time. Let's go to Gert's get a beer. I smiled. Better yet, for old time's sake …

A Piña Colada?

You read my mind.

A Third Solitude: Trespassing of the Tongue

When I decided to become a writer, I had a hard choice to make: In which language would I deliver my words? How best impact the reader? Would I write in the language of the oppressor that still roams inside our hearts and minds today, English, or in the language of my ancestors, the language of the oppressed, French?

I was raised in a strictly French-speaking home, even though half of my school life unfolded in English. Speaking French at home was a priority, something never to be negotiated. From Quebec, and living in Montreal, my parents, French Canadians *de souche,* carried with them an inferiority complex born out of having been exposed to the Anglo-Canadians' patronizing ways. They were viewed as second class citizens (for the longest while, French Canadians were treated as such: the product of Montcalm's loss to Wolfe on the city of Quebec's The Plain of Abraham, 1759—a drunken brute beating a jaded Marquis).

My parents chose to protect me from the feeling of indignation I witnessed them carry most of their life. Lowered, at times defiant, their eyes spoke loudly, at home, on the streets, and at work. The conversations that occupied our dinner table were many; of men and women living and dying with the cacophony of English scratching their ears and hearts. It was the mind, though, its posture, that was most difficult for me not to witness for from it came the spitting of words, harsh and biting—I heard them almost daily: *crisse d'Anglais. Fucking English.*

So, I was to learn English, yes, to survive, to rise to the top—maybe, like French meringue on English lemon, but under no circumstances was I to ignore my heritage, my past and my roots. My mother, whose French Canadian accent—one should *never* display such a vulgar marking—had never been heard, or suspected, often being mistaken for a Parisian, was obsessed with vocabulary, grammar, and verb conjugation. She made sure all my tenses were mastered by the age of ten, paving the way to the only trophy I would ever win: the elementary grade three French grammar award. I would give life to my parents' own ambitions, they hoped, ambitions I tried to transfer as well to my own children. They, too, would be harassed by a mother obsessed with the sustainability of the French language, the preservation of the French Canadian culture and its integrity. A pain in the ass, the annoying French sort, is what I would become in my own home.

Quebec basks in a sea of English-speaking individuals, locked in by English Canada on one side and by the United States on the other. Unsurprisingly, English seeped into my everyday life, firmly planting itself once I married an English-speaking Canadian. I had caught the virus; I had committed treason to some; betrayed my French roots to many. When I divorced from him, I swear I could have heard hands clapping and coming from my parents' couch. If they prayed to their Catholic God for me to settle down into a more respectable union, all their wishes were in vain, infertile, for as of today, my partner is from Ontario and can only speak English, his own mother tongue. Not a word of French can be produced by his brain—or, at least, very few, a true monolingual. I've tried to teach him to count past twelve ... for two years, while playing cribbage, while counting sheep, however, there is no hope. We laugh.

But am I to blame?

Canadian author Hugh MacLennan brilliantly highlights, in his iconic novel, *Two Solitudes*, the many ways in which our Canadian identity can become entangled in high-wired principles that only feeds and festers animosity. The fear of diluting our core; our origins; our purity is at the heart of this turmoil, a turmoil I never quite escaped. I think I incarnate MacLennan's version—vision maybe? of what he predicted would emerge from this conflicted identity: a new breed of Canadian. Maybe it is what I have become, a hybrid of some sort. But I am a flawed specimen, of that I am more aware; more certain; more convinced, as I float between two worlds filled with words that mesh and melt into each other to form the Gallicism and the Anglicism I have been accused of using. I seem to be unable to shake their grip. I am stuck between these two worlds I will never be able to fully please. In the end, my choice to write in English points to a truth—the heavy kind, the kind that tugs at you, nagging at your conscience. My ancestors, with their pasts, their stories, and their legacies, they are the ones I fear most. Don't get me wrong, the judgment of the English-speaking community I do fear, but to a lesser extent. The scathing and merciless opinions of the French-speaking community, whether from the New or the Old World ... well ... that causes me to question myself, my writing capabilities, my relevancy in the writing world. Do not worry, I do not discriminate in all matters, as I hope and pray for both their literary indulgences. Maybe

I simply link the words to the emotions, letting the emotions organically dictate the choice. That is what I like to tell myself. To feel better about my choice. Because it is a choice—to write in English. I simply love the language—it carries all that is meaningful to my love of writing and being. A perfect rhythm. Frankness. Movement. Coherence. I need to feel all of it when I write, and English delivers the goods—better. But the guilt is there, present with me all the time, like living with two loves and somehow pointing to a preference without leaving the other one behind. But the other doesn't suspect. No. It knows. And you feel it. A betrayal that never gets to heal.

There is a limbo, a no-man's-land, a language conundrum in which I feel caught. MacLennan was pointing to the birth of a Neo-Canadian. This, for me, points to the birth of a third solitude. One my parents helped create in me.

When I took to writing, six years ago, wanting to write a collection of short stories about my father's life, he became alive with trepidation. Write in French, Nathalie—his words, always present with me, an echo like a flesh-hungry creature.

Time passing, and he is getting older, and so I thought, well, father, here—

Papa, j'ai decidé d'écrire dans la langue de Shakespeare, celle dans laquelle tu m'as parachutée toute petite. Donc, ne m'en veux pas de la choisir ici, et surtout, sache que mes racines sont profondément ancrées dans cette terre qui est la nôtre. Ton Québec, c'est le mien, tout autant.

The stories I've written here, of these many lives we have lived, are not what you thought I'd write about, Dad, I am certain of it. I'm no engineer. Have never been interested in the physicality of that world. Part fiction, part not, these stories are born from memories that belong to that of a young girl becoming a woman, in a world of men, made for men. They also belong to the men and women, pioneers like you, that chose to live against a backdrop where harshness and levity breathed down their necks. And I apologize for betraying you with its content as much as its form, but no one ever gets to tell a writer what to write—or how to write. Not even the writer, it seems.

Never the language.

And some author once said, memory is a poet, not a historian. Because the truths that live in all our remembering are wobbly at best, subjective always.

So, I ask of you, to lean into me, French Canadian Father, trust me, for my hope is that you will enjoy reading these stories; my words, and their revelations, and that, through them, you will discover me more yet again.

For mother and sister, I wish you both well.

Nathalie

December 31, 2024

On ne revient pas de certaines impressions de l'enfance.
Elles fixent les couleurs de l'âme.

—Jean Guéhenno

Acknowledgements

Raymond Chouinard

Lucie Girouard

François Lette

Also by

"WHEN I BECAME NEVER by Nathalie Guilbeault is a haunting and unsettling psychological thriller that delves into the making of a monster and the devastation left in his wake. Exploring themes of manipulation, generational trauma, and revenge, Guilbeault crafts a narrative that is as gripping as it is disturbing. This is more than just a thriller: It's a brutal portrait of human psychology and the far-reaching impact of abuse. Despite its heavy subject matter, WHEN I BECAME NEVER captivates with its jaw-dropping twists an unrelenting suspense. It's a thought-provoking look at the limits of humanity."
— *Frank Torn, author*

"The author gives readers a poignant front-row seat to the devastation wreaked in victims' lives and the subsequent overpowering longing for vengeance and vindication."
—*The US Review of Books*

"Guilbeault is a writer to watch ... her deep dives into human psychology is matched by her power with words. WHEN I BECAME NEVER is a masterful narrative that traces the seeds of evil, and the outcome of lives touched by it."
— *Christian Fennell, The Nelligan Review*

From The
Publisher

Thank you for reading, *Cold Chaos, Stories from a North*. Should you wish to include it in your book club, get in touch, and let's see what we can help you with.

info@montrealpublishing.com

If you'd like to leave a review, that would be most appreciated, and you can do that here:

Goodreads & Amazon

If you'd like to keep up with what's going on with Nathalie Guilbeault, she can be found at:

nathalieguilbeault.com

www.ingramcontent.com/pod-product-compliance
Lightning Source LLC
Chambersburg PA
CBHW031557310726
48974CB00003B/710